Soul Cries

Wind Whisperings Publishing

Soul Cries

Written By: Lastmanout, Lastmanout@aol.com, Lastmanout @SoulCries.com

Cover art and layout By: L.A. Rowell, LdyInWoods@aol.com

Copyright 1998 by Lastmanout@aol.com. All rights reserved
No part of this book may be reproduced, stored in a retrieval system, or transcribed in any form or by any means, electronic, mechanical, photocopying, recording, or otherwise, without the prior express written permission of the publisher, Wind Whisperings Publishing
661 N. Concord Rd, Albion, Michigan 49224

www.soulcries.com
www.windwhisperings.com

Publisher's Cataloging-in-Publishing

Lastmanout
Soul Cries: A collection of musings, and
poetry on life, love and finding the path to wake
your soul and walk in the light of love
by Lastmanout. — 1st ed.
p. cm

Includes bibliographical references
ISBN: 0-615-11239-0

I. Title

PS35672.A886l37 2000   811.6
                                        QB1000-415

Foreword

All of us walk together in the hidden ways of the heart, thoughts unspoken, words measured, and walls built. Yet in all of us are the same desires, touching us, moving us, if only so we may know, as others' hearts speak to our hearts we are not alone.

It seems like only a little while ago I felt this overwhelming urge to put on paper the thoughts seemingly coming to me from deep inside and yet, directed from an outside source of immense power, peace, and love. Driving me to express thoughts, feelings, directions and the consequences of the choices we make in life. Words that brought tears to my own eyes as I wrote them. Words that touched my own heart, bringing to light feelings thought long gone. Reaching ever so softly into my own soul, driving me on saying,

> "This is the message, these are the words, write them. So others may feel the power of hope, the joy of caring, the wonderment of love, and in the end, find peace."

An awakening soul is a very fragile thing. It hurts from past pains. It aches while mending and it needs love to grow. To gently touch the soul of another can be a frightening thing sometimes. To feel another's pain, to hold it close to your heart, to surround it with love, can be an emotional bind helping us to grow stronger knowing we are truly not alone. To make peace with the past, to have the power to change the future, to feel passion, embrace life, and reach for those long lost forgotten dreams.

To that end, this is a collection of the musings, thoughts, and dreams I have been given. I know they have helped me to become more. To seek a path that has been shown to me. A path to where the light shines, where there is no darkness, where peace gently wraps its mists around all, and where we finally find all the world is truly made of love.

Of those who have read some of these musings and thoughts, one person wrote to me the following. I don't know if it is who I am. But I do know, it is who I would like to be.

A marvelous power was given one
To gaze upon tremulous hearts and see within
Misery, frustrations, hopes, and dreams, trepidations and fantasies
Desperate longings and fearful insecurities all laid bare before him
A magic dominion is allowed to touch their secret soul
To trace their spirits with presence, word, and merest thoughts
A sacred trust has been given…guardian of another's heart
A bulwark staunch to be leaned on
A trusted mentor, advisor, confidant and friend
Purposed to help another, seeking nothing for self
From those given into his protection
Not honors, nor love, nor lust, not treasure
But only the peace that comes from knowing
A heart was mended…a trust fulfilled
The master chooses his servants wisely

These are not answers but only thoughts to touch your heart, your soul. To open doors to new realities and make you think, just maybe, in a different light and open your soul.

Who is LASTMANOUT @aol.com?

Why is this written under the name Lastmanout? The calling to create, to write did not appear in my life until I began to access the world wide web. It was here I found the writings, thoughts, and ideas of all were instantly available to everyone world wide. The time, the calling, now felt so right, was right, and from my spirit the words flowed.

The world wide web is a place of screen names. Some funny, some sad. Others happy, and many describing a job they do. In some way they all seek to describe their person. Either in terms of who they are in actual name, but more often in the ways they would like to see themselves. An alter ego, a second person that can be free of the limitations of the real self, and very often, strengthening those wondrous values hidden deep in all of us for so long. Giving them a venue, a purpose of being.

The name Lastmanout was chosen for its representation of an assignment I once held, one now easily identified with the intent of these thoughts I am guided to put to paper. The Lastmanout is the person who is responsible to see everyone else gets out safely. To do whatever is necessary for those who may be hurt, injured, or lost. To let them know there is always someone there, and in the end to bring them all home.

This is the description of the Lastmanout I have placed on my world wide web site:

Who is Lastmanout

A consultant, businessman, inventor,
engineer, electrician. welder, machinist,
pistolsmith, bounty hunter, and dreamer.
A specter who walks through dreams
Coming in the gray fog bringing light to the mind, warmth to he heart
and causes the heart to know, there is a presence of peace in the world.
The bearer of joy to those oppressed and devoid of love.
Who walks in silence surrounding all he meets with a bright glow of love,
Then disappears silently into the mist
between substance and shadow until needed again.

And who knows...just maybe that is who I still am, the last man out. Only now using words to see all might still get home, but now, to their real home. Whoever I am, I hope these words bring whatever it is needed or neglected inside to light, or simply validates your ideals.

Lastmanout

My Dreams

To listen to my dreams

Is to listen to the sound of angels' gossamer wings

Delicate

Sensitive

And yet with an overwhelming force of purpose

Wishes held close

Lest my heart be betrayed and broken

For my dreams are the hidden thoughts of my soul

Fragile beauty

Wrapped in clouds of thunder

Never knowing where the lightning will strike

◆

All have all things within them, hiding there

in silent places we do not look, but only feel,

as a shadow softly and slowly passing

Knocking on Heaven's Door

The sands of time slowly pour out in a never ending stream
Each moment can be likened to but as a single solitary grain
But each grain can help to build a grand and majestic castle
Or just a part of the avalanche of tumbling sand washed away

Will you hold me for but a moment while time ticks in heartbeats
Will you kiss my eyes and cry that I may feel your tears once more
As they wash away all the pain I hold so deep within me in silence
Will you touch me gently yet leave your fingerprints there on my heart

Time flows in cascading ripples, the past, future, present all one
I close my eyes and feel the moisture bead, forming drops falling
As once more another moment of life passes in grateful harmony
Hand in invisible hand standing there knocking on heaven's door

How many lessons are there to be yet learned till the door opens
The presence of light shines out from within like a lighthouse beacon
Yet the foundation is weathered and worn bearing the scars of time
But standing, holding firm as the waves of the "who we were" beckon

Forever seeking the elusive stillpoint deep within where all is but one
Once the path is truly begun we find the stones have bruised our feet
More than your hand in mine now, it is your heart beating in my heart
You cannot cry without I feel the tears, nor laugh without I feel the joy

Yet while you live so deep with me and I within you, you are not there
You exist as a shadow of light I can see just out of the corner of my eye
The presence I can feel waiting there around the next bend, the next door
Lips softly on my cheek with a whispered prayer just before I fall asleep

Each night I go there again in dreams now, to the gates of purest gold
I worried in times past for you were not standing beside me as I knocked
Until finally I began to understand the meaning of the lessons I was given
You have always been there inside deep with me and I inside with you

It is when the gates open we will find the shadows of ourselves outside
Seeing our true selves, smiling, waiting to embrace us standing inside
Knowing now we have always carried all of heaven's love within ourselves
Needing only to knock on our own heaven's door to find it

♦

He Waits

He waits
He remembers not why
Only that he must wait here
In this place where there is not time, not space
Waiting to be filled again, for the emptiness to be gone, the search ended
Endless cycles of light…dark…light…dark…light
Waiting in silence for what seems eons,
Drained of all senses, of touch, of heat, of cold, of all but hope and love
For inside, deep inside, in places that should not even exist
Deeper than the heart, deeper than his very essence
A coal that will not be extinguished burns
It burns with an intensity unknown
That no person, no thing, no circumstance
Can diminish by the smallest amount
Through all the pain, the darkness, the loneliness,
The evil that surrounds him
Seeking to stop his light from reaching the world
That last reserve remains
Unmoveable, irrepressible, unquenchable

Now he slowly raises his head
His eyes begin to release their darkness
Deep within them begins a fiery laughing glow
As he senses the coming of the wind
The wind from the wings of angels
Finally coming again
Slowly they surround him in great love and peace
Their breath on the remaining spark he would never relinquish
Brings it to a magnificent glow
A brilliance wherein no darkness can be
No doubt, No pain

He smiles peacefully, mirthfully, knowingly
Once again he goes forward
To give again of his heart, his light, his very soul to others

So they may know also the strength of hope, of love
And in the deepest depth of their darkness there is light

He knows he will come back to this place again, and again
As with unflagging purpose he gives his light away
That slowly he will cease to be
He smiles
Fulfilled
It is enough

◆

Through the Glass

Can you feel it...searching for your soul...it's coming
All around the air is electrifyingly alive with the magic of it
Its siren call awakening those deep hidden desires within you
Needs long ignored, hidden, almost forgotten, yet always crying out
For satisfaction such as can never be found in worldly successes
Inside ever searching, wandering aimlessly, lost in the darkness
The joy of riches has faded into the lonely acquisition of only things
Better jobs, climbing that ladder of success only brings more stress
And the emptiness grows...The search goes on

Love, a family...brings a satisfaction of sorts to the lonely heart
But still, inside, that unknown hunger, the longing to be filled remains
Refusing to be ignored, it slowly and persistently gnaws away
With all there is now, the dreams come true, it somehow is not enough
And the emptiness grows...The search goes on

Faster and faster the pace of life increases seeking some relief
In the mirror you begin to wonder who it is who is looking back at you
What will it take to break down that hidden wall deep inside you
The logic of man remains all too frighteningly silent for it has no answers
Seeking only to step through the looking glass into that other world
A world where the soul, finally at peace, sings with the songs of angels
Where the longing can be set free at last knowing it has finally come home
And the emptiness grows...The search goes on

The end of the search is within, desperately reaching out to be touched
Trying to break through the wall of self direction, self fulfillment, self doubt
The directions, the signposts are there to be seen, to be felt, to be embraced
They are there in each sunrise, each sunset. The whisper of the night wind
Seen in the innocence of a baby's smile, and the laughter of children
The wondrous promise of the rainbow after the storm, always fulfilled
But only for some. For the rest remain with eyes and hearts tightly closed
Those who see, who dare to release, to feel, to trust, step through the glass
And are suddenly beyond the turmoil, wrapped in peace, in light, in love
But for those who cannot trust, whose faith is only in the world and themselves
The emptiness grows...The search goes on

◆

> Be careful what you seek to know,
>
> for sometimes in knowing
>
> you miss the lesson you were to learn,
>
> then you must repeat the experience

Silent Music

The music plays…without instruments…without notes…without sound
Wrapping around us, crescendos of majesty mixed with dark deep wails
Silent sounds playing invisible bars only our hearts, our souls can hear
The music of our lives. The marching strains of victory. The blues of defeat
Like a haunting movie our lives play out to the sound of background music
We are only marginally aware of, and none but us will ever hear or appreciate

Now, sit back. Relax. Bring to mind all the memorable moments of your life
When you were young and the all the world was yours, and love was new
Can you hear it…music of love dancing through your mind with your first love
And how the melody changed when it ended, as you thought you would end also
The solace our wounded hearts, our wounded pride found in those secret melodies
Music no radio ever played, as you drove through joy and pain, ups and downs

When you finally grew up, found your true love, you needed no music to dance
The melody raced through your head, and the voices of angels sang the words
And then when just sitting quietly, holding each other softly in peaceful bliss
Each heartbeat plucked its own chord of soulful sounds only you could hear

Then there was the time you did that dangerous thing you'll never, never do again
But while you were doing it, you heard the silent music urging you ever onward
Nursery rhymes and children's songs as you carried your newborn child home
The blues and the hymns reverberating through you in those times of great loss

Now time has passed and your life has chosen a path to walk for a while
Ah…but now…what music plays for you now in the moments of your life
The music we hear…or fail to hear anymore…is the meaning of our life
Is the silence deafening…does the music of your heart, your soul, make you cry
Or do you sing joyfully with the voices of angels with the dawn of each new day
The melodies that play for you are your own…the music of your own soul

Orchestrate your life so the music you hear is that of your own true heart
You alone are the real and true writer and conductor. The arrangement is yours.
Never let it be drowned out by the sounds of needless strife and meaningless life
Tomorrow is a new day…Come, take my hand…Let the music begin

◆

Each day will be how you make it,

how you see it,

the choice is always yours,

but know, all you seek outside,

is inside, waiting only to awaken

when you find all there is…is love

For a While

It seemed so wonderful, to be young and know the feeling of love, of being wanted, held, attended to, knowing someone wanted only you. The feeling so easy to accept, so wanted, you stay just…for a while.

Time passed and imperceptibly slipped ever so slowly into apathy. Not even noticing the lack of real passion in our busy lives, we only talked perfunctorily at each other as we passed each morning. But soon the children will be old enough to stand on their own a little and to help out, giving us time to get it back, it's only…for a while.

So many things I wanted to do, so many dreams lay in dust at my feet. Who is this person I see now in the mirror, whose eyes look back with haunting sadness? Responsibilities, yes I have responsibilities, I have so many things to do. But they seem to have no importance, and it's just…for a while.

My mind grasps now blindly for my dreams, and holds only shadows. What were they? What was it I wanted to do so long ago, so far away that my memory fails? I only wanted to find me. The who I am, not the person that someone else wanted me to be, but it was only…for a while.

Now there are no dreams, and not even a small memory of them survives, for the pain would be too much to think about what I have thrown away. I watch the grandchildren play and I see the wonder in their new eyes. I can feel the joy in their new hearts, and watch their minds majestically soar into the clouds with imagination, dreaming my precious lost dreams. And my heart screams, don't wait, don't wait, run, run with your dreams now while you still can…please don't wait…for a while.

♦

The arrogance of youth cannot be overcome

until its spirit is tested enough

to seek beyond itself.

Until that point one can only point the

direction and let the words fall silently

Soulmate

Where had it all gone, lost now, lost and distant, only a shadow remained
In memories, searching for those wonderful times, when love was new
When the moment of passion for each other ruled the very lives
Consuming, with joyous fantasies of life to come, of loving forever

The impetuousness of youth has given way to the realities of life
Dying passion can no longer fill the emptiness within the soul
The soul cries out in agony and frustration for its mate denied
Needing desperately that hand, that heart to walk with it
To know, to really know, someone understands the loss within
To fill the ever growing void with love, understanding and compassion
If only for a while, a moment out of time where the souls can touch
And merge once again into one being, complete, fulfilled, at peace

For each there is a soulmate waiting for the special times of life
Where we may chance to loose our way and our steps falter
The need, the desire to grow within one's self can no longer be denied
Your heart feels them waiting, almost with you, but not really there

Sent but to hold a hand, an heart, a dream, a soul gently in love
Physically but for a fleeting timeless moment on life's stage
The energy of light, of love, of truth…blends, binds, unites
From that moment on, to truly know…without doubt
There is love, there is peace, there is understanding
A life that has once again been given worth and purpose

Watch, lest the opportunity be lost, a signpost not seen, a path not taken
The emptiness, the longing, shall then never end
Never be diminished and the great tragic sadness would be
Forever together…eternally apart

◆

All of life is a dream,

and once dreamed is to be lived

Special Children

I watched them come into the room, mothers with their children
Some of the children with a crooked smile
Some with an arm held up and the wrist hanging
Some dragging a leg behind them slightly
Those whose eyes looked, but did not see
Those whose words would not come for they could not speak

I watched the heads of those who were there turn and look
They looked away, as if, if they did not see, they were not there
And tears filled my eyes and my heart broke

Not for the children, but for those who would not see
For in each child, there was love, bright and shining
Happiness at just being there, trust and wonderment
And each parent held a hand gently, with such great care
Leading them to see all the wonderment of life

The wonderment the rest of the world takes for granted
The sun rising in the morning was a joy to behold
Fascination watching the butterflies in all of their beauty
Hearing the quiet sounds of beauty all around them
Giving their parents new insights into the small wonders of life

Oh, the medical bills were hard, and the world indifferent
But these parents walked in such joy, for their children were truly special
And their hearts were filled with so much love you could feel it
Because these people had special hearts, warm, patient, and caring
They were chosen to watch over thoxse who need so much care

I watched the eyes of the children shine
Saw the joy of love unfolding, and I knew
Although they were the ones called special needs children
We were the ones who needed them
And I cried

◆

Dreams within dreams within dreams,

pathways there and not,

yet we dare smile and laugh and sing,

and in all the dreams as long as we love,

does it matter if we are awake

Broken Angel Wings

She watched the other angels soaring out over the heavens
Joyous in their flight, powerful wings lofting on spiritual currents
As they watched over their earthly charges with light and love
Guardian angels, each given someone to guide and protect

She tried not to be sad, for she was an angel, but a second class angel
Her one wing was broken, and she could fly only in her dreams
She wept angel tears that fell with the sound of tiny beautiful bells
Their melody so wondrous and beautiful and yet so very lost and sad
Why wasn't her wing healed? Heaven was where all things are possible
What was her purpose? She had so much love and light to share yet

And on earth, the woman looked up into the night sky with sad eyes
She had tried so hard to make it work, to make everything all right
Although there was love there, it was incomplete, distant, darkly demanding
Ever tugging at her being in ways she did not understand nor want
Making her feel trapped in the middle of what was to be total true love
Never to be what she was meant to be, the longing in her forever unsatisfied
Walking through life, searching for herself, with her own special broken wing

Their eyes met. The angel on high and the earthly angel, and they knew
This was why they were both created, their very reason for their being
With a great shout of joy the other angels carried the little angel to earth
Two angels, one of the heavens, the other of earth, now one
The glow surrounding them both was like a brilliant sun

Grasping each other, two angels each with one broken wing became whole
Soaring on high to the sound of mighty trumpets and gentle harps
Finding themselves and each other, becoming as they could never be alone

So it is with us, wondering what our purpose is and why we can't fly
For we are all but angels with one broken wing
And the only way we can fly is by embracing each other

Never let go of your dreams
I want to watch you…fly

◆

Each child is a soul, one that must learn for itself, all we can do is hold the signposts, for while the young know not fear, they also know not direction

Tears and Thunder

Valentines Day, a time of romantic remembrances, soft thoughts of caring
A short interlude in life's hectic ways, pausing for love, was fast approaching
A time to renew old vows, a time to make new ones, a time of just a moment
To stop and put aside selfish needs and celebrate the joy and majesty of love

Some find a time of great joy, for they have been blessed with shared love
For others a time to wish for joy as they tell that secret person they are loved
And for still others, just another meaningless obligation they go through
But most of all, this is a time for heightened expectations, of silent wishes
Wanting to know, needing to know, the overwhelming feeling of being loved

I watched, fascinated, as people rushed to the stores for their treasures of love
One walked through the stores hurriedly, pausing only briefly at displays
Trying quickly to remember what she would like, what it was she did like
Did it even matter. He was well-off, a fancy bauble would fulfill her needs
He quickly purchased a pair of fancy earrings thinking that should cover it
He left the store while talking on the cell phone about business and golf

Another man walked slowly through the displays, smiling as he looked
He wanted so much to find just the right gift to show how much he cared
But, alas, nothing there he could afford was good enough, he sadly thought
He could not bring her just anything, it had to show how very much he loved her
It was so hard for him, searching for a treasure on his poor man's pocketbook
Finally he realized it had gotten too late and he had still not found the right thing
Hoping she would understand, he picked out the best roses he could find
And with a heavy heart, thinking he had failed, he started slowly home

The first man arrived home to find his wife standing there with a gift for him
She was smiling, hopeful, praying, this time, let me know he loves me yet
For he had grown distant, aloof, taking her for granted, returning nothing real
He took out his Valentine's gift, "Here, this should make you happy," he smiled
She looked at him standing there waiting, not in expectation to see her joy
But waiting only to be thanked, to have his obligation over and done with

As the lightning struck outside and the sound of thunder rolled over them
Her own realization flashed in lightning and a realization in thunder came
Vows made by two to each other cannot be held together by only one

The other man arrived home feeling forlorn, as if he had failed somehow
She meant so much to him, had seen him through all the hard times
Held him when he was down and returned even more love than he ever dreamed
He walked in and saw her smiling eyes, happy he was home with her again
Holding out the roses he watched her walk over, wishing if only he had more
Tears ran softy and slowly down his cheek as she took the roses from him

She looked into his eyes and saw all the love there, love beyond any words
As her own eyes misted over, she told him, there could never be a better gift
Not the roses, but the soft tears of love telling her he was hers alone, forever
Their tears of joy, of love, flowed silently together, as did their hearts

◆

Finding Self

It is not hard to find one's self, for you see, you are always there
Inside you know who you are, yes, you do

But so often you find yourself controlled by others
And the dreams you had have seemed to slip silently away
Each day you wonder what tomorrow will bring
There are some things you must learn
Never love anything that cannot love you back
You will never see the door that opens
If you continue to beat on the one that closed
Others only control your life if you let them

No one can make you happy, but you can make others happy
If you do this you may just find you are happy too

You are loved…yes you are…we all are
The light is there to walk in, but you must go to it willingly
It cannot shine where it is not wanted

If you look, really look, the world is full of people
Gladly willing to take your hand, to walk with you
Wanting nothing in return except your joy and well-being

Love brings love, joy brings joy,
We become that which we think we are
Slowly, imperceptibly it happens

But we can choose the path
To laugh, or to cry, it is a choice

Each dawn brings forth a new day
A new beginning
A new life

And each day, the choice is yours

◆

Lost in the space between heartbeats,

where time has no meaning,

and breath is of vibrations instead of air,

silence becomes as music

and the melody plays on the soul

Cold Fire

The fire was dying, the warmth it once gave was growing dim
Only smoldering embers glowing eerily in the darkness remained

What was once thought to be the heat from a raging fire out of control
Has turned out to be only its own reflection of the fire so freely given

A fire only continues to burn brightly where fuel is continually supplied
Otherwise it consumes itself, rapidly at first, then slowly until all is gone

Leaving nothing but destruction and cold ashes in the wake of its passing

The fire of passion, of love, was given freely, basking in the return of its glow
But fueled alas, not by returned love but only by itself, it had no chance

You took love's fire, dancing in its flames, eyes laughing in the flickering light
But the fire never touched you and the heat you sent back was only my own

You walked through the fire like the person who walks on hot coals
Never consumed or even burnt, but rejoicing only in your control of the fire

Ever demanding to give more, to burn higher, hotter, consuming all
While you laughed, refining your grasp on the glowing coals of my soul

Now as the fuel is almost gone, the small flame flickers weakly in the wind
Searching, crying out for the love it needs to keep its hope, its life alive

And it knows now, it cannot, shall not, will not sustain another's control over it
For to do so any longer is to waste the heat, sacrificing a soul purely in vain

While there is one last coal left glowing, it shall remain there, untouched
Refusing to be wasted, knowing the self must be saved lest all be lost

And when true love comes, fully returning all that it is given and more
Then the fire will burn as never before, for its fuel of love will be everlasting

Its warmth reaching deep into the heart and soul, sustaining all needs

…Never give up hope…never give up yourself…You are worthy of love

◆

All must find their own self worth

and know they are love,

for if you cannot love yourself

for who you are alone,

how can another love you?

No one can make you happy, they only

increase the who you are as you become one

Dreamwalker

He walks through her dreams like a specter

Haunting, silent, an essence just beyond reach

Supplying all she needs and yet supplying nothing

Questions that can have no answers

Reasoning without understanding

He passes like mist through her mind

And softly, ever so softly, leaves footprints on her soul

And an ever lingering desire within her heart

As he vanishes like smoke with the dawn

◆

Each love lost is a lesson, a lesson teaching us,
so when the real love comes, we will understand
and be able to be to them, what they are to us

Simple Magic

I watched them slowly walking down the street, gently holding each other's hand
There was such a quiet peace about them, you wanted to walk with them
Most of those they passed smiled at them, involuntarily, without even knowing
Those with someone would reach for the other's hand, or an arm around them
What was the wonderful magic at work here in these two aged people walking
It wasn't some deep dark mystery to be learned…it was simply the power of touch

Remember, those times of your life, when just a touch meant so very much
Your baby reaching out, touching your fingers, your nose, with wonderment
How peaceful and full of love you were just to hold your sleeping child in your arms
How the touch of the hand of the person you fell in love with excited you so
To hug that long-lost friend you thought you would never see again with such joy
To be there, to hold the hand of an aged loved one and see their eyes smile

The desire, the need to be touched, held, never goes away no matter how old
It might be hidden, or sadly suppressed, afraid it shows weakness, but it's there
And to satisfy the need in another might also satisfy the same need in yourself

Try it, the results may take a short while until others realize what is happening
Within themselves as you touch them. But this is a wonderful, positive circle
Start with gentle touch and a smile just to let them know you care
A quick light hug for no reason, from behind, arms around gently, not sexually
The lips pressed slowly into the others neck, brushing the hair with a light sigh
Just giving your love, expressing it, because you do care, happy they are there
Not asking to be hugged back, just giving, says more than words ever could
Remember when you loved walking hand in hand, feeling their hand in yours
How with that simple touch you felt so safe and secure, you felt wanted, needed
Never worrying about onlookers, not caring what people would say, just content

When was the last time you touched your mate, just to let them know you cared
Such a simple thing, with such great rewards. Not only to them but to yourself
Brushed your teenager's head gently, smiled at them for no reason other than love
Don't forget the old people. Many have no one left to hug them, and they yearn
Just like all the rest of us. Touch me, hug me. Please let me know you care

Here, let me hug you, let me feel the warmth in your arms and you in mine
Come take my hand and walk with me, for I am not ashamed. I am proud to care
Remember, sometimes, when you reach for a hand, you wind up touching a heart

◆

While my friend talked, the words strained, intertwined with innuendoes unmeant to be voiced. I thought I could feel sadness, emptiness, and the loss of dignity. These thoughts came to me as I felt the being within her crying out, desperately seeking just to be heard.

Forgotten

If you hold my hand
      Should you not hold my heart

Walk closely beside me
      Do not let me walk alone

For my steps are uncertain
      The path now obscured

My eyes are on you
      But you don't look back

You walk without care, brash and loud
      While I care and walk in silence

Once never far from your sight
      Now you do not even see me

My heart remembers you
      But you don't even know who I am

Our ships no longer run together
      And have passed in the night

Now we are far from shore
      The water is dark and murky

And I fear
      I've forgotten how to swim

◆

Love is the most wonderful thing for which we can hope,

and the most difficult to achieve,

for love is subjective

You cannot love another fully, in truth,

until you can love yourself for who you are alone

For this will ultimately determine your capacity to love

Eyes Do More Than See

Eyes, the mirror of the soul, telling all our deepest hidden secrets
  Speaking far more with a glance than volumes of words can say
    And yet how many take the time to look into another's eyes
      To find the truth, the joy, the desperation, or love hidden there

As we pass each other in life, even in those tiny brief moments
  Why do we not look into the eyes of others, just for a moment
    Are we afraid of what we will see, or afraid of what we may show

All of us walk together silently in the hidden ways of the heart
  Secret thoughts unspoken, our words measured, our walls built
    And yet, in all of us, are the same desires, touching us, moving us
      If only so we may know, as others speak to our hearts, we are not alone

And yet alone we are sometimes, for we look, but we do not see
  Does the sadness in others' eyes remind us of our own
    Do we wonder why we do not have that wonderful sparkle we see in others
      Are we afraid to offer a kind word when we see the look of despair
        When someone's eyes are harried or sad, would not a kind word help

How can we expect to walk through life needing to feel wanted, appreciated
  When we ourselves cannot offer the smallest word, or smile to another
    To see a wonderful flicker of joy, of thanks, when your eyes smiled at them
      For no reason other than to let them know, you wish them well
        Can bring a soft and quiet inner joy to both the giver and the receiver

And so the question really is…what do our eyes look like to others
  Do our eyes laugh with humor, or are they sad with the pressures we all face
    Do they light up with the insight of the fantasy of the pictures we wish for
      Or do they look hauntingly for understanding, searching for unfound peace
        Each must be true, for each is true for all…the question is…

        Which face, which heart, which eyes look at us

        And which looks back at others

◆

As gently as you hold your own dreams,
you must learn to hold those of others

The Message

She knew she was dying. She had known for a long time
He sat so vigilantly there beside her as she lay motionless in her bed
Sleeping so softly, quietly, as if she had not a care in the world
The gentle breathing, the only sound in the deep silence of the room

His mind raced, his heart pounded, how does one say good-bye
How does one end all the wonderful years of togetherness, caring, love
All the bad times, what few there had been, were now long forgotten
Washed away by the soft tears of love with each ticking of the clock
Oh, for just one more second, just one more minute to spend together

Remembering the start, the miracle of how they found each
Two lost searching souls, who found each other and became whole
Running wildly, passionately through life, hand in hand, heart in heart
So close they knew what each other thought, the next words to be said
Never thinking, even imagining, it could or would ever end apart
Now the time is short, so short, each second is as precious as a year
A treasure measured far beyond the golden riches of a king's ransom

Her eyes open and she looks at him, knowing he would be there
She smiles. That silly smile that has lit his life and brought him joy for so long
It's almost time to go, silent words from her eyes touching him gently
Oh, if only he could take her place, he thinks…but then she would be watching me
Looking down at me with my same fears, longing, uncertainty and loss

She slowly reaches up, her old hands still soft, brushing a tear from his cheek
The words come to him as if in a dream, surreal, forming in his mind, his heart

"Do not be sad my love. We ran wild and free. Hand in hand we knew love
Love far beyond anything we could ever imagined or ever hoped we could have
Now I must leave you my love, just for little while I must walk without your hand
But my journey is not to be alone for you see there is an angel just there beside you
Telling me of the wonderful place I am going while I wait just a while for you.
For we were right all along. Our two souls were in all truth really only one."

As she spoke he felt a presence beside him, a presence of total love
And in his heart suddenly felt the beautiful, wonderful truth in her eyes

Suddenly the room was gone, he was standing knee-deep a in field of fog
A brilliant white light everywhere as far as he could see, and he was afraid

Then a voice spoke. A voice so clean, pure, beautiful beyond all description

> *"You have seen the end. The choice to journey there remains within you*
> *But know this, the path cannot contain pettiness, selfishness, or control*
> *Each must help, uplift, support the other in what their part of the soul seeks*
> *For although you are but one, without real love, you will be forever apart*
> *and your walk through this life will be forever lonely, in vain, wasted"*

Suddenly he awoke. He was sitting in his chair, his wife shaking him gently
She smiled at him. "You were crying softy in your sleep. Are you all right?"

He looked at her with a new mind, and new understanding, a new heart

"Am I all right
Yes
Yes my love
I am
Now"

◆

Whispers

A soft voice speaks in my mind, almost imperceptible, but always there

The time is coming…wait…wait…do not rush…I will be there…

Even with all my questions, the whispers bring a curious sense of peace
Each time my heart cries out in its loneliness the whispers come
Gently wrapping in magic all around me, dispelling my longings

…I am coming…wait…wait for me…I am your love…your peace…

Whispers touching my very soul with a tenderness I have never known
Always there, and yet, just out of reach, filling me with the presence of love
"Where are you?" my heart cries, "when will you hold my aching heart?"

…Not yet my love…wait…wait…I will come…you will know me…

Ever searching all I meet, looking into their eyes, listening for words unspoken
Knowing she is there, just around the next corner, on the next street
Tomorrow, maybe tomorrow, though I feel no rush, for the voice is strong

…I am coming…I will find you…for we two are but one…
…I am as incomplete without you…as you are without me…
…Do not find another…for then…our true longing will never end…

And so I patiently wait, a smile soft on my lips and in my heart
For those eyes I will look into and hear in my heart that silent whisper

…I am here…love forever is ours now…we are one…

◆

Illusion is a cruel refuge taken when love or
fear's dragon breathes fire, yet is it not real,
a fantasy of one's own making, for in you is
the power of all things—of all love—seek it,
feel it, for only it's real, then the world you see
is the world you make, the one in which you will live

Timeless Moment

Shimmering with an elusive, insubstantial silver mist

She walks through the recesses of my mind

A presence as soft as a rose petal on my heart

Gently drawing in my essence, cleansing it with her breath

Removing the imperfections, leaving only deep peace and love

She looks out through my eyes and the world fades slowly away

Merging her very being into mine until we two become only one

A togetherness so total, so complete, we have but one heart

No questions, no regrets, no today, no tomorrow, only now

Time has stopped and we exist only between our heartbeats

All barriers, all indecision gone, love beyond all feeling flows

We become pure love, pure light, expanding ever outward

Shinning with a brilliance, a warmth only known by the angels

The clock ticks, the heart beats but once, our moment ends

Leaving me alone, drained, empty, but wrapped in gentle peace

Waiting, waiting forever now, listening for her footsteps

Grasping for her presence, my heart now beats silently alone

I cry for my sorrow…and…I cry for my joy

◆

Each question leads to another, but it is only
when you stop asking questions that the
real questioning should begin. Never worry,
you question, only worry when the question never changes

In the Land of Time

In the land of time
Where there are no yesterdays and no tomorrows
Dwell those whose dreams walk forever through their minds
Whose hearts have chosen this moment to be forever locked in their soul
Wondrously experiencing all
Forever in a moment of infinity
Oh, how often we have all wished
If only this time could last
That moment of joy
Of laughter
Of love
Of completeness
Of peace
That so quickly slips through our fingers and our hearts
To stay forever
And not face the day to come
For we know it could never match this moment of beauty
This place does exist
It exists in our memories
A place where we can retreat whenever we wish
To relive the good times
And thankfully those memories softy beg us to continue
To make more wonderful memories
To feel good from the joy of helping others
To give love
Unconditionally
Without expecting any return
and experience the overwhelming loving presence of GOD

◆

Look not with your eyes, nor hear with your ears, but when when you find your soul is at peace…then follow that path

Unspoken Words

The silence is deafening
Each beat of the heart is felt
A drum pounding as the emptiness creeps slowly in once more
Always there
Haunting me
Even in the midst of a crowd
Washing over the senses
Draining from them all life
As the soul cries out for acknowledgment
Recognition
I am real
I am real
I am here
I know I deserve more
To find who I am
Before what little remains is lost forever
Washed away
With the stream of tears forever falling
Seeking a hand
A heart
Someone to reach out to
To be thrown a lifeline to life
A bandage for a weeping heart
To know I am not alone with my fears and emptiness
I need so much
Just a small bit of peace from the storm to hide
Hold my heart
Help strengthen me until I can walk alone
For I know not how to walk bravely through the darkness yet
If only but for a little while you take my hand
I shall learn
Then my light shall shine as brightly as yours
And then, I too, will not only finally know peace
I too, will be able to share

◆

Remember when you look into those eyes
of a child looking for forgiveness and love
if you look closely it's also a mirror in time
reflecting your own eyes

Lost Sacrifice

She loved him. But she listened to him with a soul grown heavy
Again, she was asked to do things with which her heart did not agree
They were but small things at first, and she sought to make him happy
But now it had gone far beyond that, for now he felt total control
Power that fed his ego, now out of control, demanding ever more
Without any regard for her feelings. Her sense of worth dwindled
Soon she was left, not as a loving mate, but only a thing to be controlled
It seemed the more she tried to please him, the less she became
All decisions became his. Tailored only to his needs, his wants
While she slowly sank imperceptibly deeper into compliance
Each day, a little more of herself, her being, wasted away in silence

One of the cornerstones of life is trying to please the ones we love
However, too often ignored is a basic fact, it is, it must be a two way street
There are cautionary limits of giving to others that need to be addressed
Trying to please the ones we love and others is an admirable quality
But not if it is done at the very high expense of destroying one's inner self
Those who want you to do anything not right within you own heart
Especially when you know you are trying to do right, are purely selfish
They do not have your best interests, of the relationship itself at heart
They are simply acting totally for themselves without concern for others
If you do not do what they want, they act like it is you who has done wrong
When in truth you have only done what is right, what your heart believes

There is right, and there is wrong. We call the area in between a gray area
Gray areas are only those where we find a reason to justify doing wrong
How can one expect to grow, to be at peace when doing the wrong thing
Even if we can talk ourselves into thinking we are doing it for the right reason
Is there really any difference between doing the wrong thing for the right reason
And doing the right thing for the wrong reason, both are extremely destructive

For inside we know the truth, don't we, and another piece of our humanity dies
We become like little children, hiding in the corner, hoping it will go away
But it doesn't, it never really does. We all need to find the strength to say
This is not right. You are supposed to love me. But instead you are hurting me

To force the other to see the destructiveness of their actions, their demands
To remind them when you both walked hand in hand through life in mutual caring

If the path you started on in sunlight and love has entered into darkness and rain
It is time to either find where you turned off the original path, or find a new path
Back to the sunshine where love flourishes, where you feel good about yourself
Sometimes the path will be together, as it once was. But know, people change
Those who walk not the same path, the same sharing, cannot walk together
One will walk on regardless, while the other aimlessly wanders in the darkness
When one has found the strength to know the paths have become truly separate
Then one will have started to find the true path of their life…and peace

◆

Broken Cage

I walked slowly through the brightly lit halls of where they had taken him
No longer able to care for himself, relegated now into the hands of strangers
Watching the faces, the conditions of those whose life was now these walls
When I felt a powerful presence of immense peace radiating all about me
Drawn, I went into a room where a young woman lay paralyzed in bed
The nurse smiled at me as she left saying, "She affects everyone that way"
Indian artifacts, decorations abounded for she was known as CricketHawk
I felt this need to hold her hand, to know why this powerful peace was here

Do not be sad because I cannot fly
Because you see, I do
Once I soared the heavens
Danced on the winds, lofted, floated
Now I am caged yet my heart flies
Fates have arranged I would end my life
Behind these walls
Patiently waiting, accepting, at peace
Because my soul cannot be caged
With the blink of an eye I spring upward
Spiraling ever heavenward on invisible wings
South where the fires come
East where life begins
North where your life ends
West where knowledge comes
For many years I beat my wings against my cage
Raging at the powers that took my freedom
And placed me under the control of another
Despair lit my path as I searched for a way to escape
But escape was not to be
Retreat into quiet
A quiet so deep
The only sound I heard
Was the beating of my own heart
The pain was so great
That I willed my heart to stop beating

And in the quiet, finally a voice
The voice of the Spirit
The Spirit that cannot be contained
Spirit that flows through and
between and around all things
And with eyes closed
The Spirit flowed through me
Bringing with it the fragrance of grass
the touch of the winds
the majesty of mountains
and dancing waters
And I knew that this Spirit that was
and was in all things, was in myself as well
And I spread my wings
In honor of the Great Mystery
Never bowing my head, but humbled

I walked away knowing I had been given the opportunity to share a great treasure
Given a knowledge confirming the truth of life hidden deep within my own soul
We are never so broken as when we believe we are helpless, alone, forgotten
And yet even in those times we are never, never alone unless we choose to be

I stopped by a field of flowers on the way home to reflect, to enjoy their beauty
Then I knew, life for me had irrevocably changed, my eyes, my heart opened
I watched the cars race by, the drivers unnoticing of the beauty they passed
And as I wondered who was really free and who was trapped and helpless
I saw the flowers part as if…there were…someone running through them
The gentle breeze wrapped softly around me with the scent of her perfume
As I felt once again the presence of total peace, and a soft kiss on my cheek
I knew the world, with all its distractions, could never again intrude into my soul
For now, finally, I understood what real freedom was…and in that peace
Came the knowledge…never…never again would I feel alone

With grateful thanks to CricketHawk whose words are her own

◆

With Me

As I arise, you are with me
Softly waking in my mind as the sleep drains from my eyes
Your presence in silent tune with each beat of my heart
I smile as I feel you in each breath I take
The morning coffee warms my body
But your presence warms my soul
How long had I been alone until you came softly to me
Knowing all of me instantly, in the blink of an eye
Your spirit entering my very being
Seeing deep within, knowing all there was to know
Though not there, you are, as you walk with me
You see through my eyes
You feel with my heart
Guiding my every step on our path of light
I feel a peace, a serenity, a sureness as never before
As I sit quietly, I can feel you all around me
Cuddling on my lap, your head under my chin
You slip silently into me, merging your heart into mine
Until our two souls are but one
How long I have been lost, yearning for this moment
To ever part, to feel empty again, is never a thought
A fulfillment of total love,
A giving all that is me, total, absolute, without doubt
Sharing all that I am, that I can be, that I will be
Each second, each minute, each day you stay is a treasure
And forever is not long enough

◆

The heart will lie for its own happiness,
if true or false, only when the soul is at
peace is the heart truly happy

Tomorrow

Her world stopped as she heard him come home this night
The joy of her cooking for him gone, replaced now by fear
For she heard the keys drop and scuffling footsteps on the floor
And knew there was no place to hide from his drunken rage

His eyes were blurred and yet wild with power and rage at her
Not for anything she had done, but just because she was there
All the things wrong in his life were, at this moment, her fault alone
And he thought, surely could have his vengeance on his own wife

The beating, like all the others she had endured, was swift and brutal
Leaving her bruised and battered outside and broken badly on the inside
As he passed out again, she pulled herself together for once more
She watched him as he lay in his drunken stupor, and she cried

Tomorrow, for the hundredth time, he will be so sorry he hurt her
His promises to change will again fall like rain on the desert floor
Real, wet, bringing but a brief relief and then gone without a trace
Once upon a time when love was new and he was mostly sober
Memories of the man she thought would fulfill her dreams, to love

Now, grasping to retain her own sanity, the logic of why she is there
She again convinces herself to believe he is still there…somewhere
For if he is not, then she is alone with her dreams that have died
So afraid to face tomorrow alone, thinking she is worthless
Never believing she has the power in her to be all she wants to be

And if she left….what of the children, she thinks…what would they do
In her fear she forgets…children see all that happens…and learn
The boy learns he need not respect women, force and pain rule
No punishments for anything, if you say you're sorry afterward

The girl learns women have no worth, suffering needlessly in silence
Is acceptable and to be abused is a price that must be paid

Tomorrow will be better, he promised didn't he, tomorrow he will stop
All the love she has unselfishly given has been carelessly thrown away
For she has forgotten, you cannot help someone who does not want help
Tears, pleading, and her love, fall on deaf ears and are wasted
Thrown out like trash, for they are of no real importance to him

For if he really, truly cared, none of this would be happening
Apologies and tears cannot alter the recurring facts and actions
Tomorrow, she says, tomorrow, if he doesn't change, then I will leave
The words come easy, they have come too many times before

She lays awake all night, feeling her inner fear, the loneliness of her heart
The overwhelming guilt for accepting this treatment she knows is not right
While her spirit slowly dies in this cage, the key to the door is in her pocket
For deep inside her, she knows the truth her soul cannot hide from her
She may not be responsible for the situation she is in
But she is responsible for her own actions, her own life, her own joys
She is the one responsible for how tomorrow is to be for herself, for her children
As sleep comes slowly to her now, she smiles thinking of tomorrow

>   Tomorrow is a new beginning…
>   If he doesn't change…I can leave…
>   Nothing is worth this…tomorrow…
>
>   …but if tomorrow never comes…

◆

Going Home

The sun was hot, shining down brightly as they walked to his grave. The loss was just beginning to hit everyone, awakening their senses to the loss of something unidentifiable, an awareness of something, an intangible thing they had not even known they possessed.

They had come as if beckoned mysteriously by forces unknown and they came as one. As if these strangers, from all walks of life, families and places belonged together. People he had never known were here—for he had touched many of them softly in his walk without even knowing it. They somehow knew why, and yet not, understanding only the need to be here. To each he had been different and yet the same. Reaching out to find the missing parts. To glue the pieces back together. Sometimes with reason, sometimes with logic, sometimes with humor, sometimes with discord—but always, always, with a gentle heart filled with love

While everyone else was stumbling along, trying to get ahead, he stopped. Somewhere along life's regular path, he got off. He never looked back. He went from comfortable and ambitious, to monetarily poor and yet peaceful. What did he know? Somehow never understanding him, but secretly, even unknowingly, some were jealous of the peace with which he walked. When you passed him, he always had a smile. If you asked him where he was going he would say, here, or there. But if you asked him where he was headed, his eyes would become bright and shining and with a soft voice he would smile all the way into your soul as he said, "I'm going home." He never explained. He just laughed as if he knew a wonderful secret. Smiling like a person who has given you a gift of whatever you desired most, as it was handed to you.

None ever knew, least of all him, how many he touched with his soft words, a listening heart, or a kind hand. If we complimented him, he would just smile and say "We are each given a direction, a thing to do. If taken, we will receive all that is required," so that, if only for an instant we might understand a little better.

An envelope has been passed to all of us. It is a letter from our friend…

"Do not be saddened you are here, or even wonder why

For I am sure many of you do not understand
You only know you needed to be here and can't really fathom why
Those who know, needed not come
For they understand what I've been trying to tell you all for so long now
My journey has ended and I've so thoroughly enjoyed the walk
I've smiled and I've frowned. I've loved, and I've cried
I knew both sorrow and victory
So many wonderful things fell into place once I became
More concerned with where I was headed than where I was going.

Each of you has your own dreams, goals, wishes, and desires
Of where you want to go. Who you want to be.
Just remember wherever you're going
be sure you are firmly headed in the right direction.

I've headed home to GOD's loving arms…Now, where are you headed?"

◆

A Single Drop

The small things we do for others may go forever unnoticed
Seemingly lost in the complexities of our world and our lives
But each act is like a single drop of rain that falls softly
Unnoticed. Part of an avalanche of sensory input, and ignored
But that drop, that single drop, can nourish like in all its forms
To bring beauty because the flower bloomed
To bring life because the crops sprouted and grew
To bring nourishment to the birds of the air as they fly in freedom
To bring hope as we see the rainbow in the mist after the storm
To bring faith to us as we watch the tiny miracles all around us
That are the smallest bit of the large wonderful miracle of love
All things done for others are never lost, never in vain
For even if the message or the deed was lost for the other
It was never lost to us and to the wonderful way we felt
Just to give, to help, to love enables us to know
The joy is not in the receiving
But in giving
Great things are not beyond anyone
For each small act
Of love
Of faith
Of giving
May only be the small single drop of rain
But together
We shall make a flood of love over all the earth

◆

In the moment before waking, when dreams mesh with reason, run the movies of our memories, never rewound, yet always there

Wake Up Call

He rolled over this morning and softly, gently
Reached over to caress her, to let her know he cared
His arm searches slowly for her in his half-wakened state
It searches in vain
He wakes with a start realizing no one is there
And sadness befalls him

He raises his head looking around and sniffs the air
There is no wonderful smell of fresh coffee brewing
No aroma of food flowing out to him from the kitchen
His sadness deepens as he realizes he is alone

Was it a dream
The soft gentle arms holding him
So gentle and yet ever so tightly
Bearing away the outside world
Leaving him in peaceful contentment
The soft gentle stroking of each other
Exploring the very depths of each other
Their souls melting, merging, until but one
Light, bright as the sun blazing from their eyes
The sweet scent of each other filling their senses

Was it a dream
He lays back down
Closes his eyes and hopes to sleep
Praying to hold dream once again
Experiencing the love he had found
To enter once more that world of wondrous light
Of perfect contentment, peace, sharing, and love
Knowing here, here they are both safe from the world

He falls asleep again
A smile slowly crosses his lips
And within his heart, the warmth builds

◆

It may be the older I get the more I know, and the

less I understand, but my faith in those things

I may not understand grows ever stronger

On Loss

To know the sadness and the depth of loss
Is also to know the awesome power of love
And from that love we know and feel
Although a loved one is gone
They have never really left

They live forever in our memories
In the deepest depths of our hearts
The very thought of them fills us with warmth
And we know we are not really alone

Mourn not for your loss
For you have received a gift
A gift that has eluded so very many
Love

Now it is your turn to honor that love
and pass it on lest its joy be lost
Those loved are truly at peace
Let that same peace flow softly into you
Feel it gently touching your soul
and feel the loving presence of GOD

◆

Life is but an instant in time and then we are gone, all of us, only loaned, born to either reach out or be reached to. This changes throughout lifetimes, back and forth until we learn it, and find we are all but one love

Lesson Over

Across the crowded room their eyes met for the briefest of seconds
Each felt the lightning strike of electricity coursing through their bodies
The soft rhythmic beat of each heart increased to pounding drums
In a instant they evaluated each other, clothes, hair, stance, and the eyes
And the beginnings of a wondering smile slowly crept across their lips
The mist covering the hidden longing of dusty dreams began to clear
Imagined fantasies of the heart began to dance intriguingly in their minds
Was this to be the end of what had seemed a long fruitless search for love
Others in the room disappeared from view, their eyes saw only each other
The face that haunted elusive dreams, somehow never clearly seen before
A thousand questions were asked and answered in the blink of an eye
In their minds, a golden shaft of sunlight bathed the other in a brilliant glow
While the sounds of an imagined magnificent orchestra grew ever louder
Reality long forgotten, visions of what had to be, must be, replaced all logic
The world had cruelly passed them by for too long in agonizing silence
Paying no heed to the deep canyons of emptiness ever aching to be filled
As if in a trance, they walked forward toward each other and touched
And in that instant of touch, a wondrous miracle began to occur to them
The past of loneliness faded slowly away, never to be remembered again
Any failed relationships and loves suddenly fell into new perspective
They really had just put aside their deep needs, the terrible longing to be loved
Waiting for the person they knew would come, their true love, their only love
Now the time, the moment they had been waiting for all their lives was here
For in that period, they had grown, matured beyond their own selfishness
To be able to give love freely and not lose themselves, and yet still become one
And so it is with many, who have given all to love too soon without knowing
Love is not always obtained, or even returned, just because it is given
Time can teach many lessons. Many of them hard, leaving us confused, empty
But there is a purpose, that we may learn the meaning of love, and of life
And when the time is right, the right person comes, only then we will be ready
We will look into their eyes, seeing their tears, as our own tears slowly fall
Our guardian angels will sing...for then...love will be....truly forever

◆

Each day, we have a choice, to stay where we are,
or to take that first small step into a new world.
One does not drown because they fall in the water,
they drown because they stay there

Torn in Two

The horses pawed the ground impatiently, straining at their ropes
 Like a mogul ritual, they were poised to tear the body in half
  At least that is what it felt like, what the heart in its sorrow imagined
   Was there any way back, any way out of this deep dark turmoil
    Reducing all life within to only pain and what seemed infinite loneliness
    Each day an eternal struggle between a promise once quickly given
    And the desperate need to save what little remained of the inner self
    Responsibilities crush the self, the heat with monstrous weights
     What once was black and white has now become a deep, dark gray fog
      Each day the heart dies a little more, deprived of the essence of its life

The once subtle abuses have now grown steadily into open demands
 The vows to love, honor, and cherish are now ignored and long forgotten
  A home you tried so hard to make, to keep, is only half there now
   Mirroring the self where the heart, the love is gone, but the body remains
   Responsibilities for others who need love keep one imaginably tied
    Torn in two, not wanting to stay, and yet not knowing just how to leave
     Paying the awful price for lonely security that gets ever higher each day

But in all of this there goes unrecognized an inner hidden strength
 For although one may justify and accept such a situation for themselves
  They would never, knowingly, let a child of theirs live in this dark manner
   The fight they would put up to save their child, they will not do for themselves
    Yet the children grow, accepting and emulating the way of life the see and feel
    And they come to be the very people they were never meant to be

Choices are sometimes taken out of reach by controlling measures
 Acting like mind control and after a while all things become acceptable
  The way out, the way back to reality, to one's self, becomes distant
   Acceptance of wrong, in the pursuit of what one thinks they desire
    Becomes a way of life until only the dream is left, dying and dead
     Living only in the unreal fantasy of the mind while the heart slowly dies

In all of this deep pain of the heart, this lonely turmoil of the soul
A fact goes ignored, for if acknowledged, a decision would have to be made
When one's pain is so visible, so known, and is still ignored by the other
Then only one will be forever torn in two and nothing will ever change

◆

Lost Youth

Looking for lost youth, the subject of plays, of movies, of dreams
But youth is never lost, it is only slowly hidden by the subtleties of life
We think the things that happen to us as we live destroy our youth
But such is not so unless we leave our youth where it can be touched
Where is our youth…what happened to the wide-eyed innocence of the child
Who saw everything without the heavy hand of life and fate covering it

Sit back
Close your eyes
Look into those recesses of your mind and heart
You have kept so well-hidden for years
Oh yes…they are always there waiting…
Waiting for you to bring them back
To savor them in their fullness

Now
Quietly
Remember

Your mother gently holding you with love as if you would break if she breathed
Your first ice cream cone that was soooo cold and soooo good
The merry-go-round where the horses came alive and pranced just for you
Your first kiss, soft, gentle, with its mystery now solved
The moment your love told you, yes, you were loved in return
And how at that moment in time you truly believed life could never get better
How that friend or stranger looked at you with tears in their eyes
For the unselfish thing or act you did for them
The wonder in the eyes of a child as you showed them the wonders of life
A walk in the warm soft rain holding hands
The sharing of the dawn creeping slowly into your eyes
The majesty of a sunset at dusk

All these things you tucked away in the recesses of your mind so you could relive
Those moments forever in your heart, for they were the treasure of your life

As long as these exist, the youth you think you lost is never gone
And in the moments you least expect they look out through the eyes
With the wonder of the child that saw and felt them
And the eyes begin to glow, and the heart slowly smiles

As long as we remember, as long as we can still reach out to another
With that unselfish hand of a child, wanting nothing but to help to touch
Youth is never gone. It can be seen in the eyes of others
shining mirthfully outward, sparkling with mischief, with love
If I look, maybe, just maybe, now I can see it in yours to

◆

Feeding Time

It was a hospital room. Two men lay therein, the same and yet different
Both in late autumn of their years, remembering how they had lived
One was a worldly success, rich, powerful, yet no one came to visit him
His eyes dark, like his heart had become as he clawed his way to glory

The other, just a regular working man, with only a small worldly worth
But his eyes shown bright, as did his smile, and he was never without visitors
Why, the rich man wondered, why is it am I alone…I could buy and sell him
A hundred times over and yet, he is loved, cherished, while I am despised

Finally he spoke, "I'll give you $100,000 if you can tell me the answer"
The other man looked over in sadness asking very simply, "What did you feed?"
Seeing there was no understanding in his eyes, he went on to explain
Each thing lives and grows, withers and dies, depending on its nourishment
People, animals, plants, but also feelings, compassion, hate, and most of all, love

We have oh so few hours in each day, that what we take time to feed is important
If we feed hate, then we have no time left to feed love; hate grows and love dies
If we feed revenge, we have no time remaining to feed forgiveness; revenge grows
Each thing we do, we desire, we feel, must be fed to continue to flourish and grow
If we feed a marriage, it lives, love then abounds beyond our wildest expectations

When not fed it slowly dies each minute of each tortured day until nothing is left
We can only become that which we choose to feed, that which grows and lives
When we feed our own oppression, we become even more oppressed
Or we can chose to feed freedom and life and become free and alive
We can feed hate and mistrust, or we can feed love and compassion
There is no known way to feed only one and expect the other to survive

A simple truth so often overlooked as wrongful decisions are justified
to gain personal ambition, money, fame, power, control, love and sex
And imperceptibly, by choice, we slowly sink a little deeper into the darkness
so that life becomes a treasure of earthly things and a sadly empty heart
Life was not made to accumulate things, life was made to accumulate love
Once we begin to feed love, love grows and all other things become bearable

I would rather drive an old car with my love beside me than a Cadillac alone
For one soothes my heart and warms my soul, the other only affects my ego
I choose to feed love, I choose to feed compassion, I choose to live
So now, as you look around your life, where it is, what you wanted from it
The answer may be right in front of you…"What did you feed?"

◆

Soundless Words

When we talk to God, in love, in fear, in prayer, we are considered normal
When God talks to us, however, we are perceived…well…as not quite all there
But are words necessary to understand the meaning we seek
Must we hear with our ears when our souls listen so much better
The ears often listen only to those things they want to hear
The heart listens blindly, wishing only for itself

But the soul, the soul listens with absolute clarity
Even when the ears have failed and the heart lies
For the soul knows only truth and can only thrive on truth
Whatever lies and rational delusions our mind accepts
So we may have that which we think we deserve
While the spirit waits only for those things true and
Haunts our very being with unrest until they are found

No matter how happy we say we are, or seem to believe
Until we understand the need for truth, for others, for ourselves
We find we are never really fulfilled, and never at real peace
Truth is all around us, talking to us, but to hear, ah, to hear

Words written in each sunrise as the earth warms to begin a new day
The vision of the shimmering rainbow spanning the sky after the rain
The eyes of a child, full of wonderment, trust, mischief, and love
The ability to laugh, loud and long, even when it hurts
A smile given for no reason that contagiously grows and grows
Wild flowers of all the colors of the world majestically filling a field
Their fragrance more delicate than the finest perfumes ever made
The hand that reaches out from nowhere when we are lost
A gentle touch of a friend who reached for your hand and touched your heart

I hear those things, they echo in my soul and I know I am spoken to
Each day, each moment, telling me there is love immeasurable
Hope without ending, joys yet to come, and a place just for me

Well, I am proud to be, not quite right, for I do hear the voice of God
And if you look, you can hear it too…and I'll know…for you will be
The one with the smile coming from the soul and brightening life for all

◆

All the wind's colors dance in gentle splendor
so gently in the breeze and in the rustle of the
leaves we hear the silken sounds of our heart

The Final Monster

Each day another piece of our freedom is gone. Individual rights suddenly outweigh the will of overwhelming majorities, stripping us of our dignity. Telling us everything we believe and hold precious, fought and died for is now gone. One person brought down prayer. Now other religions have more rights than those this country was founded upon. Political chaos rules according to who has the money and power. Our hands become increasingly tied to speak and the silent majority becomes all too frighteningly real. The circles of peace grow ever smaller as love, universal love, becomes only a "sound bite" without feeling or truth. The world becomes, "what can I get out of this," instead of "how can I help" and love dies. Life without love is a dream without substance and downhill we race…out of control…on a dead end road…

He was the last of his kind. All the others had been hunted down, slowly, methodically rooted out. First from the cities where they were shuffled out of existence, fired from their jobs, into homelessness where they warranted not a second look and missing persons were a common occurrence. There were no trials, there was no fanfare, no media, they just simply ceased to exist. The powerful smiled. For they knew, the people need not have real freedom, just the illusion of freedom. As the hunted became fewer and fewer, boldness set in. The media, in their zeal for political correctness now called for their extinction, for the homeless were now considered dangerous and were thus worthless. Prisons overflowed. But just for a while, yet no one ever came out. It was too late, for now no one ever questioned, even in whisper, lest they be the next to go.

He shifted his tired, hungry body into another position. The cold, wet cement floor in this abandoned warehouse sucking the very life from him for so long he had almost forgotten he had ever known warmth. He tried to sleep, but he heard the sound of them coming. He had been found. He had no strength left even to run. The crowd gathered around him, chanting, taunting him, "We don't need your kind." The pain, like a thousand needles, raging all over his fragile, starved body when the final one that would take his life hit his temple and he slowly slumped over. The final monster had been slain. The crowd quickly disbanded, like smoke from a hellfire, spreading its tendrils ever outward, dissipating into the dark night and leaving no trace of its evil passing other than a cold menacing feeling griping the soul.

The morning paper regaled the passing of the final monster, there would now be none left. They were all gone, never to return. Strangely, they did not publish his crime. When the young reporter questioned this, asking what his hideous crime was, he was told:

"Who? Oh, the monster. Yes, we are well rid of him and all like him...his crime? I thought you knew...he cared about others...and what happened to them...silly...huh...and worst of all...he knew...and I'll never understand it...how to love..."

Food for thought, or a fairy tale. Imagination or prophesy. Sleep well.

◆

Hands and Hearts

Here, let me put another log on the fire. Turn down the lights, put on some mystical music...huge fur blanket, champagne. Now come over here and lay down beside me. Let me rub your tired shoulders and look into your eyes, feeling the love that is there. Watch the flickering flames and feel the warmth as we snuggle softly together. The cares and pressures of the world outside fading away. Hear the wind caressing the house. So wild and blowing as if it wants us to cuddle even closer. And when we do it softens to the gentleness of a baby's breath.

The stars shine down through a cloudless sky, beaming the majesty of their light like a cloud over us, and merging with the flickering light of the fire. Let your heart smile now as you remember life's good times. There will always be bills, and it seems, never enough money. Loved ones may not be close and throughout time immortal, there is always a longing. A longing for something more, as there should be, touching our hearts, knocking ever so lightly on our souls, saying, "What is important, What is important...listen...listen."

Now lay back in the security of my arms, for you safe are here, and dream of the touching moments of your life. The times that held the most real, true, and lasting joy had nothing to do with money, possessions, things. They had to do with the spirit of love. Of giving to others. Not of goods. Not of things. For although they are passed, they are unimportant. You see, the joy of the gift should be the greatest to the giver. Even if the one who receives never knows from where the gift came. For to give without expectation is to give in love.

Sometimes the smallest things are the greatest gifts. The hand that lifts the small crippled child to the store window so the tiny eyes can be filled with wonder. The hand helping the old person down the stairs at the mall and carrying their treasures to the car. The hand cleaning the closet of clothes no longer needed so others can be warm. The hand that cooks the meal for those who have no fireplace to lay by and the heart that finally opens wide and gives love in a thousand little ways, maybe never even acknowledged. Those are the greatest gifts.

And as we think of those we love so dearly who are not with us in person, never, never think you are alone from them. For each who truly love are connected by golden threads reaching out form each heart to the other where ever they may be. And if you try, you can visit them in your dreams and theirs. For when your thoughts are of love, including loving yourself for who you are, then all things are possible, and nothing, nothing shall be beyond you.

As my arms wrap around you in love, may your wrap yours around others.

◆

Contentment, Happiness and Love

Content? Happy? In love? Words trying vainly to express intangible feelings that just happen to intertwine and yet, at the same time, seem often at cross purposes to each other, standing alone, aloof in our world of meanings.

When are we content, happy, in love? Surely one would think if we were happy then we would be content. But more often than not it is not so. Happiness seems to be a fleeting thing, a moment, more than a condition, although there are those lucky few who seem to always be happy. A prisoner can be content with incarceration, he suffers for his crime, but he surely is not happy. While the guard may be happy he is working but not content with what he must do.

And now we add "in love" to confuse matters even more. When we are in love, are we happy? Ah…time immortal is littered with the tales of being totally in love, but also unhappy love, hopeless love, and yet if to be in love is said to be happy and content, then surely this cannot be so. Can all exist at the same time.? All part of each other, adding to each other. Or are they separate distinct parts of our lives and inherent to what we each separately may seek? And most importantly, which is it
we seek, and which will we accept?

All seek to be in love and to be loved, but one can love the wrong person and never be happy nor content. In fact, their lives become actually quite unhappy and contentment is a luxury beyond reach. So clearly love alone is not enough and the romantic delusion it fosters only serves to bind the chains tighter on one's heart.

So is contentment enough? Can we have contentment without love? Now many, many have settled for this. They don't find the need for love all that overpowering, or have lost before and cannot stand the thought of more pain. Or they know without love they have control. But then they are not happy. Or they smile and laugh but there is no real happiness, for there is no love. They become like a beautiful bird with its home in a wondrous tree and never without food. But it has no wings and cannot fly. Its songs echo the hidden sadness of its heart. It cannot remember what is missing and yet something inside weeps bitter tears for its contentment.

Someone once asked me, "Who am I waiting for? Surely there must be someone out there for me, someone who interests me whom I could be with now, and not be alone." I just smiled. For I have watched the eyes reflect the souls of those I have passed over a lifetime. In those who say they are content, seeing them unknowingly ever searching for the briefest glimpse of love in the eyes of their mate, for that lost piece of love they know is not there. In those who say they are happy and yet are never at rest, for contentment has eluded them, and they fear love, for love will not let them keep their delusions of not needing anyone. In those who say they are in love, content and happy. Those are the eyes that forever smile into my soul and drive me onward, patiently waiting to have all three. For now, I am as happy as I need be, and I have a large degree of contentment, for I know I can wait. And she will come. As I know the sun will rise tomorrow, I know she will come. She may not even know why herself, but she will come, when the time is right for the both of us. Then we can share that wondrous merging love that brings the other gifts with it and we will know Love, Contentment, and Happiness. It is worth waiting. I will not settle, less my song echo forever mirroring that which I might have had, and been.

◆

Job Lost

Today the job was lost, the one you weren't sure you could have
You took that big chance to change your life
To be more than you thought you were
Old things were discarded and the dreams you kept hidden
Trotted out in your mind to imagine the things you could now do
You said good-bye to your old way of life, of work, of friends
And of the security you though you had, and walked boldly forward
Searching for that elusive essence of a better life

But it was not to be. The chance was gone
Gone even before you had a chance to prove yourself
And in a instant, a moment of time forever locked in your mind
Your life was irrevocably changed and a frightening loss felt

However, from this will come a stronger person
For now you are beginning to understand what you have within you
You are unique. In your abilities, in your views, in your heart
In the great scope of things there are deterrents that happen to us
Not to punish us, or to set us back, but to build us, to make us better
To help us understand, that within each of us is the potential for greatness
Not the greatness of the world but the greatness of person, of individual

The universe turns ever so slowly for some and far to quickly for others
But turn it does and in that turning comes the opportunity for happiness
Look not at what has happened, for that cannot be changed
But rather at what will happen. What you can make happen
For every door that closes on our lives another opens
The door that closes, closes because it is suppose to
Sometimes because we have learned enough in that room
Or, to force us to move forward because it is time for us to go on

Now your strength can grow, your hidden dreams can be pursued
And you will find the light does surround you
It always has, but some were afraid to look, to act, to be fuller

Each sunrise brings a new day, a new life, a new path
May your step on whichever one you now choose be firm
Filled with the knowledge you can succeed, you can be at peace
And that in all things there is some good

♦

The Wind

Ever so slowly the wind comes as if in response to an unasked question.
Soft probing breezes seeking out this darkness that should not be.
The Wind finds him, swirling around him and lifting him gently upward
As he stretches out his arms as if in surrender and acceptance.

The Wind softly fills his lungs with joyful breath
the same joyful breath it gives to the newborn child and puppy alike
The Wind caresses his eyes gentle with the air that passes through infinite beauty
The daily awakening of each day and the glow as it begins to sleep and all therein

The Wind lifts his hands, curling madly around one with the air of creation
Of strength, of the energy it has touched while the other hand is ever so lightly
Brushed as the touch of a butterfly, the softness and gentleness of a baby's breath

The Wind lifts one foot with the restlessness air of adventurers, explorers and those
Whose riding of the winds bring new things while the other is in the willing grasp
Of the air of those who stayed and built the permanence, the places to come home

The Wind fills one ear with the sounds of sorrow, the crying of the tortured
While the other ear is filled with the sounds of joy, the crying of the saved
That he may know there is not one without the other and the Wind that brings
The hurricane also brings the cool night air washing away the pain of life

Now the Wind is in his blood, racing, pulsing to his heart
The Wind that has seen, felt all there is
And understands the awful depths of sorrow and awesome heights of joy

And now a smile comes slowly to his lips, his eyes begin to glow with an inner
Light of knowledge and strength and from deep within he feels love

The Wind tumbles joyfully over the land in laughter
Lovingly and softly kisses his lips and is gone

♦

We exist as vibrations, some in tune, some not, harmonies and discords, music touches the vibrations we are with its own and joins to touch the who we are…or the who we seek to be

The Questions

There are so many lost, alone and confused souls searching for answers
Reasons why their lives seem so out of control, reeling in confusion
Unable to grasp the subtle realities of their situations and surroundings
Seeking desperately just a helping hand to guide them back to reality
How did they get this way, once vibrant people, now lost, unsure

Other people have made you this way, twisting your reasoning, responses
But many like Freud have now been exposed for the true perverts they were
Their logic based on some truths but altered to their own specific perceptions
Psychiatrists probe thoughts, seeking a textbook definition for one's actions
Oh, it is true we all are affected by the world we live in, how we were raised
And in extreme, and even some subtle situations it can truly warp someone

However, I find it strange the most asked questions to really help are so simple
Focusing the responsibility where it first started and where it most belongs
"Why do you think you reacted that way…" What do you think about it"
If when we're angry, we would stop reacting in anger for just a minute and think
Why am I angry, why do I let this make me mad, taking control away from me
A car cuts you off, you rage at the driver. The line at the market is too huge
A thousand other simple things each day raising your impatience, your anger
Things you can do nothing about, your anger, your energy, is only wasted

Why am I hurt? Is there a valid reason, or just a petty selfishness of being
You give a gift, in your joy, you thought, but your gift was not well accepted
Quickly the joy of giving is forgotten, because you wanted something back
Then it was not a gift and your hurt is wasted on your own selfish need

Life is like this, we do not take the time to find out why we respond as we do
We react blindly, becoming all important to ourselves, forgetting all others
The important questions, simple ones, they tell us much about ourselves
"Why did I do that…What do you think…What did that accomplish"

It takes only a moment to ask, and inside, we always know the answers
We have just closed them off because we really didn't want to hear them
For to face all the truths about ourselves, our actions, our very reasoning
Would cause us to have to change, be at peace with others, and maybe ourselves

Of course, I could be wrong…hummmmm…"Now why did I do that?"

◆

Each journey is unique, we are unique and
yet all part of oneness, it is only when we find all
are love that love's golden threads wrap around us
and we forever smile

Somewhere in our lives we have all met one just like this...

Femme Fatale

She came into the room quietly, clinging to his arm
All eyes turned to look, captivated by her lilting laugh
Their looks were rewarded by the sight of her charming smile
Dressed in light frilly clothes that left little to the imagination
Her hungry eyes searched the room, taking in everything
We all knew there was no loyalty present in her heart
One arm was as good as another and many would be offered
And it was plain, she was only out for what she could get
Her smile beckoned, enticing a word, a touch from any stranger
I watched as she cried out for attention that so quickly came
A drink was offered to her and she greedily emptied it quickly
She seemed totally unashamed of showing her base passions
It mattered not to her if they were young or old, they were fair game
She handled her power and charm deftly, as if unaware of it
But there was no mistaking who was the center of attention
There were those who would say she had a heart clean and pure
While others wondered just what would become of her in the end
To say, I can change her, I can make her happy, give her direction
She projected an air of helplessness that left many willing to try
But if the relationship began to stink, would they turn their noses
Running the other way as fast as their legs could carry them
But as I watched, I knew, she would get everything she wanted
At least for a while. And that is, I guess, as it always should be
For she was one of a kind, a unique personification of love

...And only two-months old

Too many search for truth outside themselves;
There is no truth to be found until you
know the truth is to be found within yourself

The Missing Element

And the world was made. Green grass, beautiful trees, sunshine, moonlight, animals and birds of magnificent order. Then came all the people to enjoy all the abundance and beauty therein. But something was missing. An intangible, fragile yet powerful essence was, somehow absent.

Ahh, yes, that was it…what was needed yet was the wind. The wind to blow over the earth, searching out all things, touching all things with its silken fingers and mists. Bringing the soft and gentle rains to cool the earth and bring life-giving energy to all things that they may rejoice even further in their being. To give the very birds of the air a cushion on which to rest. To move the clouds in their billowy majesty around the sky. To give wonder to all things in its soft caress, touching each gently on the lips and in the heart with her message of love.

And so the Wind was created, powerful beyond belief but gentle as a feather falling on the skin. A constant reminder of loving power and grace, moving elegantly over the land, seeing all, washing away our tears, and entering our hearts with love.

♦

Each love lost is a lesson, a lesson teaching us,
so when the real love comes, we will understand
and be able to be to them, what they are to us

1000 Pound Snowflake

Yes,
  I heard it
    The sound of a snowflake softly falling
      A 1000 pound snowflake
        Twenty feet across
          Rushing at me
            Through the night sky
              With the sound of a runaway freight train
                The snow reflecting the moonlight like a bright falling star

                With my name on it
                Headed for me

Thoughts of a cold, white, squashed future loomed nearer
 I bravely stood my ground
  Too scared to run
    I pulled on my gloves
      Put up the hood on my coat
        Accepted my fate
          Looking up, watching it come closer
            Then, at the last minute
              Words flashed across the snowball

                GAME OVER
        Deposit another quarter to continue

          I walked away laughing
      GOD has a marvelous sense of humor

◆

The need to forgive is only there for those who seek forgiveness,
one need not seek to forgive who walks in the light of love,
for it comes without conscience,
freely, and it moves on like a gentle breeze

Small Thoughts and Observations

Love is both the most wonderful thing we can hope for
And the most difficult to keep, for love is subjective
You cannot love another fully, in truth,
Until you love yourself for what you are
For what you are without another ultimately determines
The capacity to love and to survive with another

◆

The heart waits in silence, feeling all things but love keeps no score
For the acceptance of one's love puts all small things in perspective
None can be all that the other wants or needs
But by putting one's own needs aside for the other
They will find, in the end, their own needs met
Beyond their fondest dreams

◆

Trifles pale, when one knows they are loved
The actions of love speak in majestic terms
That words alone cannot begin to express
A soft caress at the right time
Is more important that the finest present

◆

Each day seems an eternity of strife, work, aggravation
Draining my senses and putting blinders on my spirit
But as you welcome me in your understanding arms
And your love wraps ever so softly around me
The pain vanishes, my spirit soars, and my heart loves

◆

Life is always changing, evolving, and we with it
To begin to know one's self is to begin to know peace
And with peace comes the sharing of that peace
That others may not stumble or lose their way
So in the end all may be all they choose to be
And more than they ever dreamed

◆

You come into my dreams softly as a shadow
Like a touch of a feather, and stay there forever
When I'm not in your arms, you dwell in my soul
Dispelling my loneliness and making me whole
When I can't feel your lips, you still touch my heart
And then my spirit understands the full joy of love

◆

Time is fleeting and though we must learn from the past
The present is all we have to enjoy, to build on, to be
Life is far too short to carry burdens best left behind
To take the hand offered, to be a friend, to care, to love
All we are becomes more with another

◆

The passing of time accelerates and the memories it brings
Seem sometimes like only fleeting glances over the shoulder
To live each day to make the memories stronger is to be alive
To see the hidden treasures in even the small things that make life
So wonderful and then to willingly share them will make memories
That will warm the heart forever—for then they are truly made of
The bits and pieces of the love and times that are our lives

◆

She just found out he was cheating and it felt like her heart stopped
Tears ran streaming down her cheeks and her soul was in agony
The heart that once held so many dreams was now only an empty shell
Did he know how devastating this was—did he even care at all
What did it matter now, now that trust had crumbed into dust
Was his pleasure worth the pain it caused. Only he could answer that
But no answer could justify the loss of the love once held so dear
And pledged forever as dreams vanished, and a heart broke in two

◆

It is too quiet. He longs for another to be there. But one comes
For he has chased them all away with brash words and his come
on attitude. Now he is alone. So very alone. He can hear his heart
Slowly a tear rips from his eye and splashes into the floor as he sobs
When will he learn, love come gently and quietly to those who wait
But runs from those who wildly and randomly pursue it selfishly

◆

I can see you in my mind, an ethereal being surrounded in light
Soft shadows of infinite color rising around you
While you cast golden threads of joy outward in vain
For there is no one there to understand how to hold them
and they slip silently away

◆

He is gone now. The house echoes with the emptiness of it.
She thought this was what she wanted, free to do as she desired
But somehow now it feels lonely and sad.
As he walks away, the same feelings come also to his heart
Both of them wondering why the other never listened to them
When they both sadly realize, they were too busy talking to listen

◆

The melody of joy touches each thing on its own level…but the notes are universal

Wind Chimes

In the soft twilight stillness not a sound dare disturb the quiet
The sky streaked with the paint brush of red, violet, golden rays
Stretching as far as the eye can see, and the mind can dream
Thoughts drift as slowly as the clouds as the fire in them dies
Memories, dreams play on the darkening panorama of fading light

Softly, from out of nowhere as if silently beckoned, a quiet breeze
The night wind comes to wash away the last vestiges of day's chaos
Caressing with a lover's touch, delectable, succulent, and addictive
The eyes close to fully enjoy the mystery of the feelings aroused
And then, like tiny little angel bells, the wind chime music begins

Their resonant rings harmonize with the peaceful place we have gone
Gently tolling their random music better than the finest musical score
Blending with the heartbeats of dreams and memories once hidden
Melodious vibrations reaching ever so gently to blend heart and soul
A whisper of peace and belonging brings a mellowing of all there is

It is in this place, this time, I feel your presence in the wind chimes
A memory as soft as the chimes in the whispered wind all around me
And as beautiful, the random melody reaching deep into my heart
Bringing the same peace, blending your music and mine into only one
I feel your touch on my soul with each musical note played by the wind

As the wind dances, the wind chimes dance, and the memory dances
Dreams begin once again to be dreamed and sent out with the wind
So they may mix with all the other dreams riding on the night breeze
And the wind chimes of hearts everywhere can know dreams still live

So when in those quiet times you hear the wind chime notes played
And you may wonder why they echo far into your own hidden places
It is because each note softly played is a part of someone's dreams
A chime, a bell, vibrating ever so gently but each note filled with love
If you listen close you can hear them sing, even when there is no wind

◆

The notes of love dance silently on the wind, gently touching the skin with their melody while the soul slowly breathes them in savoring each note as we dance to the tune…and learn

Will You

Will you miss me when I'm gone
When you no longer hear my voice
The quiet footsteps I make in the morning
So as not to disturb you as you lightly sleep

Will you miss my body, there across from you
Sitting at the table, eating the same meals as you
Listening always to the words you haltingly speak
As if there might be test later, a form to fill out

Will you miss the sound of my voice
Did you hear in it, all the love there was
Reminding you of this and that, and of us
Were the words enough to reach into you

Will you miss the sight of my face each day
Where eyes looked out and reached out
A face where in a history of life was written
On the smile, or frown, and where tears ran

Will you miss the touch of my hand
How often it reached out to just be felt
Brushing yours gently as if saying, I am here
Waiting just for your fingers to somehow find mine

Will you miss my arms, how they once enfolded you
Wrapping you within all the love I could give
Offering you a place safe away from the world
Where you could rest softly in them unafraid

Will you miss my heart, where love is to be
Do you ever wonder if it skips a beat for you
A sacred place within connected to my soul
Where there should be peace and contentment

Will you miss my love I tried so hard to give
Even in all those times when it was not returned
It was all I had left to offer, even when in vain
I held it out to you and watched you crumble it

Will you miss me when I'm gone?
Or should I ask, Do you know I am here?

◆

And Now What?

He had been alone for a time, a self imposed exile from the world
Past times slaying the dragons protecting windmills he tilted against
Had left him now—empty and unfulfilled as the air the blades churned
Love to had caused him such pain for he had once loved without doubt
And now all the pieces of remembrance hung like weights on his heart
It was as if he had simply chosen to stop here in this place in time
Neither swimming forward or back, nor sinking, but safely anchored

Finally the world sat there at his fingertips beckoning him to play again
Then, as he began to reach out to faceless people with strange names
Knowing, somehow, he was able to touch their pain, feel their sorrow
He began to understand what a precious gift had been given to him

It was then she first came. She knew him in her mind and she found him
Tentatively reaching out to see if he was as real unto her as she thought
He instinctively opened to her, freely, wholly, without holding anything back
Here, his heart said, I give you such love as I have to give without regret
And she came again, and again. Each time reaching deeper into him
Amazed by the clear purity of the love she found there without agenda
She began to touch his spirit, to journey with him and to open his soul
Higher and higher they went, deeper and deeper they dove, now as one

He began to live for their times together when they would lovingly merge
Two souls, two hearts, as one, feeling all the other was and the love there
Like a flower blooming, blossoming, he grew, expanded touching love itself
He did not know the reality of it all for he gave freely and she fed on him
Wrapping herself around him, driving him to heights he had not known

He was so wonderfully full of love he said take all you need and more
I need nothing back he said, and truly he did not, for his love was pure
Then slowly, as tears fell, he began to know, all was not as it seemed
She had come only to feed, to use, to take, as she had so many others
But she had not counted on his pureness, for when he found the truth
It mattered not to him of the energy of love drained, but only the reason

In growing, in touching the face of all love, he had become forever changed
He would give freely of his love without any regret, as humanly possible
For he yearned so himself for her to come to just once more touch her love
Like a drug addiction, waiting for his fix of merging oneness into all love
He finally realized, it was he who generated the love he so deeply now felt
For it had always been there inside him, inside all of us, hidden away
Waiting for the time, the moment to set it free, when it could be only free

Then she was gone. He had gotten too close to her, and she feared him
Not for any harm he would do, for he could not harm her for any reason
Though he was now love, his emptiness without her grew, consuming him
For all the things that had happened, this was still a wonderful thing to him
He found the face of love, had touched it, merged with it, loved with it
And in doing so he had become so much more than he had ever dreamed

But he also was, in a strange way, crippled forever now for the same reasons
No longer could he be satisfied with those whom he once could have been happy
For he knew, yes knew, what total love was. Love far beyond the bonds of flesh
And never again could he settle for any less. That is the pureness of his love
And while she goes on and finds others to draw love from and then to feed

He knows it is good she is gone, and for his heart's sake never to return
But in those unguarded moments where he remembers as she was to him
Tears slowly form and fall and he knows, he prays, the phone will never ring
And he also knows he would give all he owns to hear her voice just once more.

◆

This was written for a friend who was at a loss over the way his children have begun to treat him disrespectfully and with arrogance. It has left him angry at them and at himself, for his love never wavers, only his patience.

Consequences

I know this is a strange time for you. New hormones are causing emotions and feelings very new to you and amplifying the normal ones you have. You are striking out now, blindly, trying to find who you are becoming. Trying to break the bonds of our guidance. Believing you are old enough to make your own decisions, you get mad at our rules and regulations. I have thought hard on how to explain to you there is so much you have to learn still and the rules you must yet live by are not for your control, but for your learning and safety.

If I could tell you one thing I pray would reach you, other than you are truly loved always, even though at times my patience is sorely tested and at sometimes even lost, it is this: "For all things there is a consequence."

It is as true for me as it is for you, and for everyone. Everything, every single thing we do has a consequence or reaction. Sometimes it is good and then sometimes not. Sometimes it is not an immediate thing but surfaces later and can affect a life in little ways or totally change its direction, but there is always a consequence. You do not recognize this, I do, so I must protect you.

All life is a set of rules. The ones you must live by in your growing years are so very mild to the ones you will face as you grow. The decisions you make will affect your life in ways you can't even imagine at this point.

Why are there rules? Rules are there for guidance so you learn to be a part of the world without hurting others or yourself. So you might learn compassion is more important than money, that truth will come out at some point no matter how well it is hidden now, that responsibility builds character, that selfishness and pettiness will not be tolerated, that one's word is truly worth more than gold.

For all things there is a consequence. But hear this and burn it into your mind now, for it will serve you well through all your life. Most consequences you will face are of…your own bringing. If you choose to disobey, to be arrogant, disrespectful, you cause the reactions. The true depth of them you may never see for the selfishness you do, you may not see your Mother's or Dad's heart break. But you will see their reaction as they enforce the rules you chose to break. Rules there for your own good to teach and to protect. The same rules they had to learn, for they know the consequences, you do not.

Do not be fooled by the seeming short term gains of selfishness, or of actions taken in anger, or ego against others, of pettiness, of lying to get your way or to get you out of trouble. It may sound silly to you now, but we who are older have learned the universe does not forget. Sometime, somewhere, all we do comes back to either haunt us, or to reward us. Each day of life is a lesson. Life is never about what happens to you, but is always about how you react to it.

When your parent says, "I hope your children grow up just like you," it may not be a compliment…and then it may be…I guess it is your choice.

◆

"I"

How many times have we watched the children in their assurance
When the time for questions begins to slowly end and now they know
In the midst of this time comes the absolute reasoning of their minds
Some smile at them and let them have their ideas and childhood dreams
While others try to correct them, telling them why the sky is really blue
Where brothers and sisters really come from, but they do not understand

For this is the time of "I," the time where ideas begin and shape us all
Where one is in their life depends on where their "I" is and how full it is
Imaginary friends are real, they can be seen by eyes that do not see adults
And who knows what angels or others they may really see in their world
It is us, who ourselves were told they didn't exist who then stopped believing
Don't you sometimes wonder if you could have kept the angels and friends
If only someone else had also believed and seen them with eyes of true love

So we grow, and all we believe and we know, we absolutely, truly know
Changes as we progress through life and see beyond the space of self
It is like getting your nose up against a huge picture and seeing the flower
That is all there is in your field of view, so of course that is all there must be
Then time passes and you take one small step back, and lo and behold
The flower is in a field of flowers, more beauty to be seen and assimilated

More time passes and you step back farther to see the hill the flowers are on
And then again to see the lake next to the hill, suddenly the world is huge
With each of these happenings the "I" that knows and believes changes
The "I" in each begins to see how much more is involved in life's beauty
With each step back, seeing more comes fear the "I" is no longer important

Time begins to run now, the view of the flower fades into the distance
The view is huge now, almost overwhelming in its vast intensity and power
And the "I" wishes sometimes it could go back, touch the flower once more
Some go only so far and begin to build a wall, so they cannot see any more
Afraid to find the strength deep within them to keep going and touch the sky
Others run so fast, the picture now becomes only a small tiny remembrance

Some can look back and see their footprints stopping to smell the flowers
Drinking from the cool streams of knowledge put there for us to slowly savor

Each "I" walked the path making it uniquely its own, choosing its steps
From ancient times the directions to find the right path were always known
But in each person is the "I." The I want this, I want that, I want her or him
The ego without which we would not be unique unto all the other millions
Or, far too often the lack of the "I" letting subservience become life's path
And from that point on the "I," the ego no longer can say, I believe, I want

I have watched many people and all the things that happen to them in life
Births, deaths, love found, love lost, love denied, deliberate wrongs and rights
So many things touch the body, ravage it, hurt it, but pleasure it at times also
The heart may be full, or broken and torn for a while, eyes cry joy or pain
But in these things there is always the "I" making a choice to be or not to be

The "I" in each of us can be, at the same time, so very very powerful
And yet as delicate and fragile as the soft silken wings of a butterfly
For without both there is no strength and there can be no dreams
The "I" stands next to the soul and shows it the growth it has achieved
Or not, as the case may be. It is a delicate balance of ego and love
Without the loving "I" the soul is forever unhappy and cannot grow
With an "I" too strong, demanding and controlling the soul begins to cry

But the most amazing part of it all that I have found may be a paradox
Where the "I" is the strongest, full of love, compassion, and peace
The word "I" is seldom if ever heard from their lips, their heart, or soul
And when it is heard, it seems to be in the soft sentence of empathy
The words soundlessly from the eyes or spoken on the lips "Can I help?"

◆

Love or Lust

Love or Lust? Why does it have to be either/or, should it not be an and? Everyone lusts, whether they act on it or not. But not everyone loves. At least not to the degree of giving all of one's self willingly to another in trust. They qualify love, put limits on it, on themselves, demanding certain returns.

The once youthful dream of sacrificing one's all for love dies a quick death in reality's harsh light, and yet...it is a death of such sadness. For not only the image of love crumbles, but the self is left with only pieces of what it was. For in love are all the good things, trust, sharing, compassion, absence of fear, and many other attributes found only partially otherwise. Oh, there are those who show these things, but without love, real love, they are only shadows of all they should be. And in times of stress or personnel fear they are quickly compromised. But those based in real love remain steadfast in these things.

Oftentimes, love is a one way street where one person will love and the other will receive yet the roles are never reversed where the recipient becomes the giver of that very love, a far too real scenario in today's world. Not because it is right, but because it simply fills that need. But the need will grow, for the acceptance is not real. There is a piece missing within and it haunts. It taunts. More, more, why am I not happy, content, I have it all, and I am loved. Never knowing one cannot find that elusive internal peace without giving all of his or herself. In trusting another with all you are, you have no power over them. But power over others is only an illusion, a mirror of the power one fails to have over themselves. You have only the power, the control another lets you have. At any time it can stop. Then there is nothing. For within is nothing and the tidal wave of emptiness consumes all.

This is where lust begins. For lust is never of sharing. It is never of concern for the other. Lust is self-serving. And in one way or another we all do it. For things, for people, for status. Saying look at me, I have it all, when in truth you have nothing. For without love, life is a dream without wings, where each day the sun still shines and life goes on, but the gentle breeze of peace never seeks you out. But desire, raw and never ending haunts each step, each turn, while you stand there, knee deep, in the middle of the stream, crying out in desperate thirst.

Do we lust for those we love, I sure hope so. For in combining the two, we put a whole new meaning to lust. For, within the bonds of real love, lust is a catalyst. It amplifies instead of negating. It joins, instead of keeping separate. And best of all, it remains. It is not blown away in the morning like the ashes of a now cold and dead fire. One that burned far too hot and consumed all far too quickly. It is a spark with real love, ever glowing, only waiting to be fanned once again into an inferno of mortal passion to match the spiritual passion always there.

◆

I Only Know

It seems there will always be so much left for me to learn
So many new things will forever be far beyond my grasp
Science and technology together march on relentlessly
Yet for some things there can be no rational explanations

Rain falls because there is great excess moisture in clouds
Thunder forms from the masses of displaced air rushing together
I only know walking with you in its soft mists cleanses my heart
As angels' joyous tears fall and the lightning of living strikes us

The sun shines and gives its light due to chemical reaction
The exact amount of time it takes to arrive here is known
I only know the beauty of a sunrise takes my breath away
That the warmth sent over light years makes flowers grow

For the body there must be a huge system of nerves and senses
They let us hold utensils and tools and do such great things
I only know when you touch me there can be no explanation
For the feeling of peace, of acceptance, of such love flowing

The eyes see images of what is somewhere in front of them
Relaying accurate pictures for the brain to identify and use
I only know when I look into your eyes I see what eyes cannot
Your warm and loving soul shines out from them seeking me

The arms and hands can hold tools and build mighty towers
Yet paint works of art both of great beauty and of great pain
I only know when I feel your arms wrap around me, I am home
When your hand touches mine to hold it, all fear is now gone

There are so many things in the world, both for good and for evil
Material things acquired and held, treated as if they were treasure
I only know there is no amount of wealth of things I could ever have
No earthly treasure could replace one single moment spent with you

Of all I have learned, of the things I have found in the time I have been
I only know...the only thing worth anything...and everything...is love

◆

Time brushes all of us with its beauty

leaving eyes that learn to see another's soul

...instead of their own reflection

Ships

A step out into the world, a pause in time
On our way we pass like ships in the night
Strangers somehow brushing by each other
Your eyes reach out and touch me softly
And yet lightening energy crackles within
Worlds swirling with life's creation in each
Then changing to questions unanswered
I watch fires explode and then slowly die
Waves of pain and sorrow engulf my being
And then hope pours like a river from them
I am swept away, lost, drifting in the current
An invisible touch of fingers, of arms held out
Asking "Are you the one, the one I hear, I seek"
I am immersed in the brilliant light pouring out
Full of wanting, of finally finding the one to be
My heart cries deeply for I too know that feeling
I cannot breathe for the power of the wanting
In a space of a second we flow into each other
And then you are gone, continuing your walk
Turning, hoping, I search the crowd to no avail
You are gone, truly like a ship lost in the night
Searching, as I, for the light of your lighthouse
Where love's light beams out with forever fire
As I continue on, I smile, knowing I am not alone
And at the wondrous gift to someday be given
When we can both find the eyes answering back

◆

None are truly lost, they are only unable to feel the strings of love reaching out everywhere

Somewhere in Time

A liaison, relationship, love exists in but a small moment of forever time
They are the expressions and learning each needed at that given instant
Often I hear people cry they will never find love, and yet they already have
Forgotten in their moment of loneliness are all the times they were in love
Those loves may not, and evidently did not work since they are alone now
But think back, were you not alive, dancing on air, living on fragile dreams

Those times passed and the love turned bad, or left, or in some cases died
Not more than a moment, a single blink in the ever falling sands of time
If we learn from them, of the good, the bad, reasons shown and those hidden
When it ended, how many never choose to see the race was worth running
Saddened, refusing to learn from it, seeking only revenge, savoring their pain

Ask anyone about what happened to their love and the answers are interesting
Few will say how the other person did anything at all worthwhile for them
And hauling out their martyrship tells you only of how much they gave and gave
It may be true in many cases, but when that is all one sees, they are blind
No mater who's at fault, fault is always shared, if not by action, by acceptance

Paths somewhere in time, we travel along leading us to where we should be
Some tread lightly, some rapidly, while some stop, frozen in their fear or pain
How strange we think each seemingly perfect person could be "the" soulmate
When the paths must cover many lifetimes of learning, of being, of growing
Yet how can we expect to grow if others do not take our hand, seeking or giving

On this journey how much you were sure you knew when you first fell in love
Somewhere in time, a first love came to you and somehow touched your heart
And you began to soar on wings touching the sun with your fairy tale dreams
Yet as positive as you were, it ended for any of a 1000 reasons first loves end
Your freely given heart broke into a million pieces and for just a time you cried
And then, wonder of wonders, it mended when a new love for you came along

In the midst of it, you never thought of the good things you learned about yourself
Did I fall in love for the right reasons, or for reasons I can't define any longer
Will you be doomed to repeat this type of attraction to this kind of person

Is the flaw in you, or was it them, or just maybe you were not walking alike
Each in a different place in their life thinking this is what I need, it feels good
Or here is the person to rescue my poor aching heart and make me whole

While you are in one place in time, the one you wait for is elsewhere in time
Each of us are vibrations in time, as we speak and think we create ripples
Reaching out touching all others as they do us, gentle ripples of love, peace
Harsh waves of hate and revenge all wash over us and toss our soul about
Waves cleansing, or drowning, or loving, but all of them forever affect us

Somewhere in time we meet others we may have touched before on the path
Rekindling a good experience now finished with its lesson, or one not done
And although it many feel "right" it may be only familiar to the souls within
Each love lost is a lesson, a temporary soulmate only a lesson teaching us
So when the real love comes, we will have hopefully grown within our spirit
Then we will understand and be able to be to them, what they are to us

The universe watches, sees the path you walk out there, somewhere in time
And it helps to prepare the perfect person for you by guiding their step in time
So each will grow, learn what love is and when their paths finally come together
They can finally walk together, hand in hand, sharing until the end of this journey

It cannot be any other way, if walking at different rates, the arms stretch out
Until the holding hands must let go and another path in time taken by each

So what to do? Remember all of life is a learning, of seeking spirit not things
Your heart was only broken if you fail to see and feel the lesson to be learned
And although lessons are sometimes not very easy, think about the alternative
Would you want someone who has never known, touched your kind of pain
Would you want someone who has never given of love as you have given of it

They're there, somewhere in time, waiting just for you for the time of meeting
Do not try to hang on to the ones you are passing in spirit, or passing you
Embrace the life, the light they bring out in you, that is then yours forever
Walk gently savoring your time always testing it to see if it is what is to be
The one meant for you will be there…somewhere in time

◆

The Voice

Have you ever just sat there quietly day dreaming
About nothing in particular, random quiet thoughts
When in between the pictures you hear the voice
Sometimes from so long ago and now so far away
Or from just yesterday, but again, now so far away

It may whisper nothing other than just your name
But like the grand opening curtain on a stage play
It rips open your memories laying them bare to see
You cannot open your eyes, you do not want to
There are pictures playing inside like move trailers
You are trapped now, almost in a coma-like state

It seems so strange somehow as you watch the film
You cannot even remember to bring home bread
But now you remember even the smallest details

The voice speaks and the vibrations touch your heart
You willingly sink deeper into the coma of a dream
There, a quick touch. Ever so gentle, almost missed
You can even feel it. The silkiness of fingers so real
And the ripples it starts flow throughout to the heart

The voice speaks, your very soul welcomes the sound
Peace flows over you as if standing under a waterfall
Washing down around you drawing off all your sorrow
There in that place, with the voice, is only pure love

Every detail is fast forwarded in that timeless moment
All you see all you have gained, and all you have lost
You see and lovingly embrace all of that which was real
While all of that which was not real just no longer matters

The feeling carries you along, your soul has been touched
You want to stay here forever, to never open the eyes again
To live in this moment where it is all real just one more time
Yet end it must, for it was but an illusion born out of learning
A refuge taken when love's dragon breathes its fiery breath
Consuming all you are so like the phoenix you may again rise

As reluctantly you open your eyes, and the pictures fade away
You can hear the voice, like a siren softly calling you to stay
Tears flow gently, slowly down cheeks falling into nothingness
You silently pray, next time this journey will be real and forever

◆

Time and Place

In the dust, out there on the horizon where the light shimmers in ghostly waves of slowly rising heat, a figure appears, there and yet somehow not. He rides a pale horse with eyes of fire. Sparks fly from black diamond hoofs as they strike the rocks. His hat seems to pull a shadow over his face no matter which way he turns yet you can feel his gaze as it sweeps over the land and pauses ever so briefly as it touches you and then is gone. It that moment you feel both a shudder of coldness as if all of your life was there, suddenly laid bare for all to see and all the secrets stored in dark boxes now dumped and lying at your feet, and strangely a warmth you cannot deny begins from that place you have kept so hidden deep inside and its flame grows until it threatens to consume your very being, hope now begins to awaken .

He is there in the time when the barbarian hordes were laying waste to the land, when the mongols senselessly slaughtered thousands, and again in the times of the crusades when evil ran disguised as light and justice hid its face. He was there as new worlds were changed and claimed by the force of might, and time and time again as needed when truth died and compassion only a word unsaid.

From out of no where he comes silently to do what must be done, sometimes the pale rider of death bringing retribution to the evil, by a warlock's club, or the shining lance of the knight, or the soft flick of a poncho and the sound of gunfire. Even repelling down from the sky.

Sometimes only the gentle presence of the meek who does not turn away from what must be done, and who, lying beaten and battered, raises up one more time to hold out his hand, his heart, and offer up himself in love to make a difference. He shines his magic light where darkness hides and brings the spark of truth and love to those who need it and then like a flickering shadow as the dawn brings a new day is silently gone, back to wherever it is where his kind wait for that call tortured souls and hearts make in their silent screams.

He chooses not to live in a time, but for all time, and yet not, for he lives not for himself but only for others, and as he is called, he comes. And yet, one cannot but wonder what is it he thinks as he rides in, and what is it he must truly feel as he rides away again...alone.

◆

Trash

Trash, The refuse of life's use, of things, of places, of time, of people. The sweepings and debris of our lives now worthless and discarded. Or are they? When does trash become trash? Was it always trash? One of the important journeys though life is the recognizing of garbage.

Being able to see all things for what they really are is a learned process. Each person, depending on how they were brought up, their own beliefs, their own desires, how much of themselves they are willing to sacrifice to have what they think they want, designates their own level of "acceptable" trash.

The teenager who is soooo attracted to a wrong person because they are soooo cool, sooooo bad, or so good looking, considers that level of trash acceptable. Later as they grow they look back and wonder what it was they saw and why.

Those who marry a drunk, an abuser, or a druggie because they think they are in love, or for any other reason, consider that level of trash acceptable. Their selfish heart says, it is ok, I can love that person enough for both of us. But lies cannot live forever, it does not work out and hopefully the light is seen. What was once acceptable can now be seen as trash leaving one to move on.

Those who stay together because they think they have to, for the kids, because they cannot afford to leave, because the other person is ok half of the time, or simply because they are afraid, again raise the level of trash they are with to being acceptable. And in doing so, lower their own self worth even more.

Recognizing life's trash is directly related to knowing one's own self worth. All are worthy...of love...of being treated fairly, with dignity, and respect. Of being able to express themselves without fear, and a thousand other things. The more self worth one finds within themself the less trash they deal with. For once they identify trash they will not let the trash interfere in their lives. As one's self worth grows it becomes easier to identify trash for what it is. For trash shows no one respect, not for others' opinions, nor for their lives.

Trash is only interested in tearing down, gossip, belittling, using, and lies. Unless you do not believe in yourself and they are telling you what you want. Things you think you need to hear to feel important, part of the clique. At that point they are not yet trash to you. They are your acceptable things. It is only as you grow in seeing the truth of life, of yourself can one recognize them for what they are. Listening to the warnings of others does not help until one begins to feel their own self worth and begin to trust in that self worth.

Trash. Users, the abuser, the lier, the cheat, the gossip, all serve a purpose. They are some of the ever important lessons of life one must face in growing. How can you ever know what you are worth until someone challenges you. It is how you stand up to the challenge that determines the trash in ones life. The more you challenge things, and believe in yourself, the less trash you have.

How do you recognize the trash? Anything, anyone whose actions are not in total concert with the laws of good, of the love in all things, has only their own interests at heart, not the good of others. These things are the trash of life. Trash should be disposed. For the longer you keep it, the more it smells. And the smell lingers, touching and affecting all who happen to be around it.

But all this can only be seen once you accept love and your own self worth. For in the end, what you see and accept in life you will see also in the mirror.

◆

A Walk in the Park

A normal day, or so it seemed, as she strolled through the park
The spring weather bringing forth its magic rebirth of all things
Sunlight brightly streamed everywhere warming the land with light
Laughter rang over the fields with young voices once again at play
Couples of all ages walked by slowly, hand in hand, heart in heart
While others came to just sit, to watch, to hope and maybe dream

She thought she could pick out the ones remembering times past
Looking out, not seeing the scenes there, but the ones in the mind
She too had pictures remembered playing warmly times long past
Often, long ago she wondered what things she would bring to mind
In the time she hoped would never come, when her love was gone

So strange she thought, sometimes I swear I can feel him almost here
Watching over me still with that mischievous smile and laughing eyes
How wonderful he had always made her feel with just a gentle touch
Their time together had been far too short and yet somehow it still lived
Others over time had come and gone and been cared for a just awhile
But he was the one she remembered in the quiet place only she went

Their time had only been but a second of life's wonder in all of eternity
Like a brief encounter in a movie scene where fate directed the meeting
Knowing not even why it was happening, but only that it was happening
Strangers and yet not, for they had felt each others being touch them
Drawn together without thought for in this time and place, all was right
Peace and love flowed slowly around them like a river engulfing them

She could feel now his gentle warm touch in the sunlight's soft rays
A soft breeze washed over her and back as if he was there breathing
She picked a red rose from the flowers there and held it to her face
Remembering how softly he would kiss her eyes, like rose petals
Then almost in slow motion wrapping his arms around her with his love
There, in those precious moments, all was as it was ever meant to be

Was it worth it, someone once asked, to love so much for so little time
And she had smiled then and felt sorry for the person who had to ask
For she now knew, if only for a second of time's wonder, she was whole
For there truly was another who understood all she was, and was not
If they had never met, never touched, never kissed, never held each other
She would have never really known the depth and passion of true love

She remembered the question once again, and her eyes began to smile
Her heart was young once again, beating with her dancing memories
As the sun caressed her once more, the wind blew his breath on her
She walked slowly away holding her rose to her cheek as soft tears ran
And her heart, her soul, and her lips said, "Oh yes, oh yes, oh yes"

◆

Reaching

Picture in your mind a hand, any hand, plain or delicate
It does not matter what it looks like to anyone but to you
The hand is not connected to anyone, just a hand and arm
It is open, slightly turned, fingers spread, curving, reaching
There is nothing around it, only a silver softly shining mist
It can be coming down or up or sideways, anyway you want
Have you got it, fixed there now as you see it in your mind

Now, the question only you can answer. What is the hand doing
You have there in your mind now, the reason the hand is reaching
As surely as you have made the picture, you've made the reason
The reason however isn't imagination, it is an essential part of you
A reflection of something inside you called forth now without thought
Just as in your mind you already have the reaction you would make

In living and observing life through the eyes of one slowly awakening
I have found many reasons a hand is put forth, reaching for something
At many times in our lives we reach out, either to help, or to be helped
Hopefully this changes back and forth over time so that we might learn
One can never always be in need, nor always the one who must help
Learning to help without selfish thoughts, or to be helped without pride

Yet there are those whose thoughts turned to neither of these reasons
For when a hand reaches out to them it is a hand of pain or accusation
A hand of control seeking only egotistical power, keeping fear instilled
Or maybe the hand is reaching out in anguish, frustration, apprehension
Strange how we change over time, as for whatever reason, reaching

The new child reaches out to touch and experience bright new things
Its tiny hand is open in the trust of the very young and very innocent
The criminal reaches out to take from you not only goods but yourself
Invading the who you are, the world you live in, dragging you into theirs
The lover reaches out ever so gently, so softly, to just touch their love
There, in the stroking touch of the hand, of fingers, love might be felt

What memories come back to you now, of a just a hand, reaching
The remembered clasp of a friend thought lost so very long ago
The hand pulling you to safety, or your hand pulling someone else
The hand threatening you, or your hand threatening someone else
Or maybe like one I fondly recall of just a hand reaching to touch
Gently holding hands as we walked, side by side, down the road

So now, remember, I ask you why the imaginary hand was reaching
Your answer may be an insight into who you are and how you are
Was the hand reaching to yours for help. or yours reaching for help
Did the hand mean pain, or control, or freedom from both of those
Full of love and innocence, or filled with pain, hate, greed or envy
What is the reason you first gave as you saw the image in your mind

Is there a moral, or perhaps a lesson hidden within this musing
Or am I just...another hand...or heart...reaching...for yours

◆

Star Song

The sky was like black velvet, so dark and warm
A robe of cushioned silence stretched out forever
The twinkling of fireflies in the night's summer air
seemed as bright as the twinkling of distant stars
Light, thousands of years old still calls hauntingly
With a beauty undefinable and somehow magical
Pulsating and breathtaking in its exquisite power
No moonlight shines to intrude on the stars' songs
Each star playing its own wondrous silent note
The eyes take in the melody written in the heavens
As it plays on the heart the soul weeps to the tune
So small now one feels and yet somehow not alone
For if the very stars reach out to you their message
then you too must be part of all there is, of their song
Comets rush in, their tails made of dreams answered
Rushing earthward to bring someone's fantasy to life
And in the mind the words of a daydream song linger
"When you wish upon a star" and then you too wish
The stars flicker as if in answer to castles in the air
In this time of quiet, of dreams, of silence, of peace
If you close your eyes and watch only with your heart
You can see an endless flight of angels in the heavens
And you know, now, and for all time, there is love.

♦

There is no spirit without humor, the ability to see laughter is like seeing love in each sunrise

How Long is Forever

When the words speak I love you
Then how long is forever
When you speak the word soulmate
Then how long is forever
Playing in my mind, in my heart
We made each other smile, laugh
Places in heart we shared, touched
Were they two souls for a while one
Were the words from another world true
Not a coming together at all
But continuous flow that has always been
How long then is forever
A choice to make, a path to walk
Yet is it destiny or choice we make
We care not where it may lead
As long as it is together we share
Hearts, minds, souls, love
How long then is forever
Is it in the passing of the moment
A speck on the line of time's journey
Never knowing why we do as we do
Things without logical reason
Against human reason
Sometimes it is enough to know not why
But only to know we would
We must. We will
Then hearts will understand, savoring
How long is forever

◆

Times touches each in soft patterns and with them is an essence of being each carries in memories, recalling them as needed at those times when the heart needs to smile

Longing

Time slipped by so quickly, he thought
Here it is, the Easter season once more
Even in his rushed life he knew one thing
He better remember to bring something home
A gift to let her know he had remembered her
Her love was chocolates, unfortunately his too
But he had recently given them up for his heart
And he wondered if he would have the will power
To go into the chocolate store and not sample

She smiled slyly waiting at home, for she knew
Subtle hints dropped did not fall on his deaf ears
Only on holidays would he buy the really good stuff
The chocolate melting, lingering on the taste buds
Almost as good as a sensual soft and longing dream
She waited in anticipation to see what he would bring
How much trouble he would take to bring the right thing
She knew he could not eat it anymore and she knew
how much trouble he would have not to eat any of it

He walked around the chocolate shop in a daze
The air filled with the overpowering sensual smell
Every cell in his body came alive and began to crave
His pulse raced, his eyes began to slowly glaze over
Oh to be locked in here, alone, for just one single night
He quickly wiped his drooling mouth as the clerk came
"What would you like" the clerk smiled sweetly at him
Inside he cried out "ALL, I want it all" but he said only
"Some really good fancy chocolates for my loving wife"

She found her heart thumping as her anticipation grew
Hating to put him though all this trouble just for chocolate
Chocolate he could not, or should not, any longer eat
But she smiled, it was not that often she got the Godiva
And wasn't she now making his very favorite meal anyway

She vowed to at least eat them out of his sight, alone
Where she could slowly savor each melting precious one

He left the shop, forcing his feet to move, one more step
The perspiration of longing beaded on his forehead
And he let out a long sigh of relief, or was it submission
He smiled as he looked at the box he had them wrap up
And wrap tightly and so pretty so he would not be tempted
How much trouble had this really been for his will power
And yet, he seemed happier and somehow fulfilled now

She saw him coming up the walk and spotted the box
Her pulse began to race at the thought of his love for her
How much trouble this must have been, how hard for him
But here he was and there was the box she so craved
She took it with hands she hoped he did not see tremble
Promising to sample it out of his sight so not tempt him

He was happy to make her happy, she was worth it all
Although the fragrance of the chocolate shop still lingered
And he involuntarily began to lick his lips of the moisture
Loving chocolate as he did, he knew he bought correctly

She was alone. She opened the box ever so carefully
Gazing on the varieties inside, so many, of all types
She slowly began to touch, to taste the wonders therein
The first layer now gone she removed the divider
There were a just few special chocolate pieces missing

She knew she had to forgive him his own longing
Smiling she knew it would not be a hard thing to do
It would be just like the box of chocolates she held
Absolutely…it would be
…no truffle at all

◆

Purpose

In a field, on the side of a hill, quiet solitude, time to reflect
It is growing dark, the night closes its curtain over the day
The hot dry winds slowly change to a cool moist breeze
Sounds of daylight are replaced by the night shift awakening
The woods are alive in melody with tiny sounds of tiny things

Slowly the field comes alive with thousands of dancing lights
Fireflies play in ever shifting patterns, a kaleidoscope of beauty
On the breeze the fragrance of night flowers lingers enticingly
More subtle and precious than the finest of perfumes ever made
Each breath savors the flavor, the taste, too delicate to describe

Above, the stars begin to twinkle out their light like tiny ornaments
As if hung with invisible strings and arranged in timeless patterns
Each sending its message in flashes of light across the universe
Somewhere in the distance a plentiful howl echoes over the hills
You can feel the sorrowful power of the cry vibrate deep inside

The moon silhouettes the beast on the hill, or is it a shadow of us
From that hidden place where we would howl, if only we could
Shadows seem to shift and change, becoming figures and things
Ghosts of things dreamed, ghosts of things held, and then let go

As the night grows deeper and the stars brighter, you feel smaller
Wondering, how in all this huge majestic wonder, of your purpose
And from the night sky the Coyote Lady laughs her silken laugh
Holding out her hands, beckoning you to come, to see, to know
With this your spirit can now soar, riding the winds like an eagle

Your eyes now see with the sight of your spirit, awakened at last
Angels come and go, filling the sky with heaven's majesty of love
Some taking souls home, some bringing new souls to start again
But all the souls are smiling, laughing, joyful in their experiences
Gathering around you, touching, you suddenly know your purpose

You smile and you're back in the field looking up at the heavens
The fireflies come and dance all around you, you can feel their joy
Creatures of the night come just to be petted and rub against you
You raise your hand, smile, reach out and touch one of the stars
As its light, traveling for centuries, shines all about you with its halo
Peace, like an ever so soft blanket, wraps gently around your soul
For you now know your reason for being, your purpose in life
It is just to…Love

◆

The Answer

It is silent now, the sun set long ago, the night sounds have faded
Half awake, drifting in and out of thoughts both hidden and those real
There is no conscious thread aware of, yet there seems a direction
Imagined background music plays to the mind's scenes flashing by
In this state we are aware of being watched by an ever loving presence
We reach out with our thoughts and dreams seeking an elusive answer

A path, a direction into dreams or a path back from free choices made
Thousands of years beyond youth's age when we absolutely knew it all
Time has gentled both the rage and the headlong rush into fools land
Here on the edge of the land of sleep the mind and heart remember
Foolish choices so often made for those reasons both good and bad
Learning has come slowly, painfully, the only way it could and so last

In the surrounding silence you can feel the loving presence of a smile
No matter the age, the experience, here in its glow all are but children
Slowly the knowledge begins to bathe us in its warm beckoning light
As we agonizingly watch children make mistakes so they may learn
So it is with the free choices we are left to make, to feel consequences
Till we finally learn, those decisions made in selfishness, lead us away
Oh how hard it is to let go of the small worldly things we think we want
And so be able to receive all the wondrous gifts we were meant to have

The soul smiles as we lay there, for the answer has finally been given
Peace of such deepness never before felt settles over as sleep comes
As love smiles from above, the cloud of knowledge drifts slowly away
It trails out until only a single thread is left connecting as morning dawns
For some it is enough, they grasp the thread and hold on for dear life
A remnant of perfect peace and love now lives in them, they find a new path

While in others, it is only a haunting memory they cannot hold on wakening
Refusing to give up their dreams of power and wealth never knowing the truth
Power over others is only an illusion, a mirror of the lack of power in one's self
For only when you hold the dreams of others as gently, lovingly as your own
Willingly sharing all you are, do you find they all come wondrously true

◆

Peace comes silently on angel wings as one takes that first small step to know of things we cannot see…but only trust are there

The Gift

The Christmas season had once again come on angels' wings
It was a time of rejoicing, a time of reflection, remembrance
The fragile beginning in such great love, that it would never end
A time to give our small gifts now, as great gifts were given then

In a room grown shabby, yet warm, over time as finances faded
Old eyes sparkled with a magic glow, like seeing a star at night
Here in a worn creaking frail body a heart was wonderfully alive
Having known many things on a long journey now nearing its end
A smile of quiet peace you knew was gained finally, at great cost

What to do, the old one wondered, on a pension's meager funds
Most of the friends long passed on, the children distant and quiet
How to pass on all the feelings not only of the season, but of life
The smile grew slyly bigger as out came plain paper and pen
Old eyes strained and the hand shook as the words slowly formed

In another room across town, in a huge house with many servants
Young eyes also sparkled, bright, twinkling like light off a diamond
The excitement of the time of year flowing through like electricity
Here the body was young, playful, the heart open and innocent
Awaiting its own journey to find, in time, its own path to life's truths

What to do, the young one wondered, daddy was rich, what to buy
Something to make mommy's, daddy's, friends' eyes shine like new
But wait, small eyes remembered the times of their short new life
Seeing great gifts given become as dust, for here something lacked
Yet at poor friends, small gifts brought sparking eyes and warmth

A smile beamed on the young one, it was Christmas, it was easy
I know just what to give, and it will be for everyone, one size fits all
The smile grew slightly bigger as out came colored paper and crayons
Small eyes strained and the hand shook as the words slowly formed
The tiny heart leaped and danced as each one was lovingly printed

Both rolled them up, put them into tiny boxes and drew a heart on it
One put on an old worn coat and then slowly hobbled out with a cane
The other a bright coat and hat, roller blades, then skated out the door
Both looking to give their presents not to those with smiles, but frowns
For both time and innocence had found the same quiet truth of life

Each handed out their box with a smile and shuffled or skated away
Leaving the person wondering what had happened and why to them
They opened the tiny box and pulled out the note and began to read

One note was laboriously written by shaking old aged hands in ink
The other laboriously written in shaking new hands in bright crayon
Both said the same thing and each note seemed to glow with energy

*"You may think this box is empty, but is not. Inside is placed the
only gift I have of my own worth giving. I do not know who you are
I only know you looked like someone who may have needed this gift
You cannot refuse it, for it is mine alone to willingly give to you
It did not cost anything, yet its value is beyond the ransom of a king
It will keep you warm. It will cause you to smile. It will bring peace
But if you hold it only to yourself it will slowly wither and fade away
Yet if you freely share it, it grows so big you cannot ever contain it
Inside this box, is my love. Just for you, so you know, you are loved"*

Around the corner the young one came narrowing avoiding the old one
They looked at each other, saw eachs boxes, and somehow they knew
The young marveled at the love and the peace found in the old ones eyes
The old one marveled at the love and the innocence found in young eyes
As they hugged and laughed, standing just behind them, angels smiled

Somewhere between the innocence of the very young and the peace
of the very old lies a journey of a lifetime to find what we always had

◆

Here is a portion of a reply I sent to someone in a group when questioned about relationships and happiness, why they thought they were missing something, and why they hurt from past or present relationships. This was part of my comment, maybe it may give you some insight.

Relationships and Happiness

Surely most all have been in a relationship where it was "comfortable" for lack of a better term, but somehow something was missing. Nothing you could put your finger on, for surely the person you were with loved you. Isn't that what you were looking for, to be loved? Or was it? How many people have relationships only because the other person fills a gap in their lives? They are loved, and they convince themselves they love back "enough" so it is alright. But somehow it isn't, the nagging inside taps and taps and taps on you silently, saying, "Is this all there is?" You have what you thought you wanted, or did you just let the hole in you be filled? This is what so many do.

For some it is enough. For others it is not. But where to question? Where is the fault, the cause of either, the acceptance, or the longing? Before we look at the ones you "let" love you who do not totally fill the hole, you must first step back and take a look at yourself. It is one thing to say there is something missing. It is another to say, "I know what is missing," and then to identify it as missing in them, or in yourself. Where is your "need" really coming from?

Most people have so many unresolved issues they are not even aware of, some imprinted in their upbringing, others as they grew in acceptance of what they thought was the right way to act. And lots, out of the relationships of youth where hormones raged and anything was acceptable to get one's end. From all these things, few people, however strong and independent they seem, have come to that place where they know and understand their own real worth.

In learning life, falling in love, and out of love, one hopefully progresses from the love of physical attraction in youth and how important someone is because they have a beautiful person next to them, to real relationships. The problem with real relationships is that they *are* real, others expect things you may or may not be prepared to give, and hearts get broken, used, abused, and the walls go up.

As common as this is, this is the wrong reaction. Oh how wonderful it would be if we all found the right, true and lasting love the first time. But how can that be when all of us have to learn, in our time, in our way, to overcome selfishness, pride, greed, possessiveness and a hundred other normal faults—to be the person the OTHER person deserves? Each lost relationship or lost love is not a failure. It is a lesson (about how other people are, yes) mostly about how you are. How you choose to accept the happenings of your life. What did you really learn? Not of the "poor me, I'll never do that again and put up emotional walls."

In each love gone bad, was there not a wonderful time? As one said, of the sacrificing your life for another if need be. How much more, how much more wonderful could a feeling be? You open up and say here I am, this is me, I am opening up so you know who I am, and it feels sooooo good. So now that a relationship may not be all it seems, does that make the feeling any less wonderful or important? NO, of course not. This was part of your opening, of learning about your ability to open, to love, to be more than you have been. Is there still more to learn when you find you have been hurt? Why of course. You need to learn why you have been hurt. What is it in you that really hurts? Only pride. The great gift of being able to love is still there—and better than it has been to you in the past—to be used, to be cherished, to be held out again with open arms.

Is there a time and place to be careful? Why of course there is. But you see, IF you learned, this is now slowly becoming an instinctive thing. For only when you can give real love can you detect real love. Those who would have used you in the past will no longer be a part of your life, and if they are, then you still have things to learn. You see, it is all is part of the plan, the learning, the loving of not only the one you ultimately seek, but just as importantly, of yourself.

So if you feel there is something missing, first find out where it is missing. If it is within self, then that person can never be totally happy and the hole in them will remain unfilled. Communication between each is important to solving this problem, but again it must be allowed to be self-examining. And this is where defensiveness begins. It becomes easy to just accept things and not see what we choose not to. Life changes all of us, and most do not change together. But here also lies a trap, and one of the comments that left me "uneasy," where it was said someone HAS to talk about everything.

There is a fine line between sharing lives and maintaining one's own identity. It is wonderful to be able to talk about "anything and everything" but do you need to? Are there not those parts of each that we keep to ourselves? Not with an intent to hide them from our mates, but only to maintain the core of our identity. For without it we have then nothing to share. "Becoming ONE" is part of a time we share, willingly, never to be dragged from us. It is both a natural thing and yet a thing at which to be worked.

I have been there, where the bonding was complete, so far beyond the normal acceptance of becoming ONE. I have truly seen with her eyes and breathed with her breath and she with mine. Spirits merging. And yet, as real and true as it was there in the moment, it was not to be for long, yet alone forever. Yet there was nothing lost. Oh, my heart ached badly for a time, until I came to know this was the most wonderful lesson I could have ever had. For it was now I knew I was capable of a level of love far beyond anything I could have imagined. And I could give this love to others, and love myself. I could never build a wall now, never to say you cannot see the "who" that I am, for it is the who I AM that now can truly love.

◆

To be hurt is to expect more from one than is given,
to forgive is to realize you wanted something back,
to go on is to hold only the lesson…and let the rest fade

The Movie

He slowly blinked away another small tear flowing from his eyes
His weathered cheeks were wet now with tiny rivulets of soft moisture
Down one side trickled the gentle golden tears of love once touched
While on the other side flowed the red tears of sorrow for love lost
The mind racing ever so fast now even while his breathing slowed
For his time was almost over now, time measured only in minutes

A movie of his life, in glorious wide screen technicolor passed
Wait! Stop! his heart cried. Go back! Let me see more clearly
But the scenes only slowed in important moments, never stopping
There! His first love. Seen again now but with eyes grown old
Both the wonder and innocence of all he was then tugged at him
Now with the awareness of aging years he was able to see truth
The pettiness of youth's selflessness never meant to be, but there
Yet this too was, he now knew, only one part of his lesson to learn
Sorrow at his actions so long past and forgotten overtook him now

Again and again it seemed the same lesson played on the screen
Different times, different ages, different players, but the same lesson
Until it finally became learned and changed him so he could move on
Oh why, his eyes cried, had I not seen what was right in front of me
So much wasted time spent refusing to acknowledge who I was then

The movie slowed more now. Sensing the change he became alert
Important parts, the ones where a path was chosen came slowly now
He saw himself change with the lessons and his heart began to open
Not with the false opening and tiny selfishness of opening only to one
But slowly, like a flower to the morning sun, just one petal at a time
Opening willingly to the light, savoring its majesty his soul did likewise

He saw the times fighting the human demon seeking to drag him down
Selfishness's voice once had haunted him, tearing at his conscience
But with an opening heart came an unbeknownst peace surrounding him
And as the soul began to open and then smile, finally came understanding
There exists only a shadow of the real life when the heart remains closed

Dark mists where love is only rationed for both logical and illogical reasons
A place where a return of some type is demanded before any love is given
Or the specter of the self sacrifice accomplishing nothing raises its ugly head

His breathing becomes slower now, labored, gasping and yet he smiles
The heart pounds, erratically, madly within him now but he feels it not
His eyes, his very being, riveted to the scenes still passing before him
There was so much yet he wanted to do, to share all he had finally found
He had opened his heart and then held it out boldly for all the world to see
Hiding not the tears of loss or pain of the lessons he said here look, look

We all choose, each day, with each step, the very lessons we are to learn
The lessons to teach us life is nothing, only a misting shadow, without love
Sad tears fell as he thought of so many he knew only one small step away
From finding the doorway to themself, a door away from fear, control and pain
Yet so afraid they will not take that step to be whole, to be free, to be loved
Their world becomes living in a shadow where they were never meant to be
Love is all the wonders there ever were wrapped around you in forever peace

He tries to write down the answers so others can read them, but he can not
The fingers will no longer hold the pen to paper, his strength is gone now
Tears flow uncontrolled as his heart cries, I must tell them all, I must, I must
They need not know loneliness, or loss, only loves peace if they only open

As his eyelids slowly close, he hears the sound once more, a whisper
The one always there for him but just somehow out of sight, out of reach
Wrapping around him, she becomes him and he knows she will never leave
As their souls rise in peace and joy, a voice of all love speaks silent words
"Come child, you have learned I am forever there in every heart, every soul
Yet each must find their own way to learn to open their hearts and find love
The gift has no lock but only the one they themselves choose to place on it
The need only believe they are worthy of all the love there is, and it is theirs
Flowing over them without price, or control, or fear, only free then forever"

As the words faded the sky became alive with golden shimmering light
The very air slowly breathed in became as haunting beautiful soft music
And although no credits scrolled across the sky, I knew love's author well

♦

The Opening

Words from nowhere, yet everywhere

Whispers and cries from deep inside

Like a flower slowly beginning to open

Layer after layer delicately pealed back

And with each layer the beauty grows

Vulnerable now in its fragile fullness

Yet there is no more fear any longer

No pretext or falsehood can now exist

The heart and the very soul lie open

All you are is now to be seen

All you are now is to be shared

All you are now is love

You are Free

◆

We rage not because of what is done to us,
but because we refuse to accept the lesson in what was done

Veils

As if in a dimension out of time I watched the figures passing
Faces faded away leaving the only recognition of them an aura
A shimmering of their being, of the hidden who they really were
Shades of ever varying light and color, no two exactly the same
Yet some were brightly shining while others were dull and dim
Most perplexing were those who carried a mist surrounding them
It was like trying to see them behind a veil, a curtain of unknown

For some the veil was bright, glowing, as if it to were itself alive
In these the veil was clear, translucent, cracking with an energy
The faceless figure striding confidently as with great intent, purpose
I touched this veil, felt the single dream carrying this figure forward
Yet noticed none other could reach through to touch, to hold this figure
And the mist created was also far too dense for the figure to see out

I sought another, this time not quite as bright but glowing beautifully
Here also the same energy sang, but the melody was slightly different
Alive, but with a softness the other did not have, it glowed deeper
Touching this one I also felt the dream, but here it was many dreams
As others came, they not only entered the veil but left also shining
For here the dream was dreamt in good for all and its strength grew

I sought another, this one a golden soft glow just wishing to be touched
The figure in this one peaceful beyond any measure, or any description
As I looked out over the horizon there seemed to be so many of these
The depth of glow varied but the warm inviting color was always the same
Touching this one, uncontrolled tears began to fall for this one was Love
All touching it left with the start of the glow spreading slowly over them

I sought another, this one like a gray fog, one single small light within
The figure here seemed strangely out of place as if hiding inside
Hesitantly I touched it. There was no feeling, it was there, and not
Then I understood, this was a veil of illusion, without any substance
Here the figure hid in their own fear, their own lies, afraid to question
Never knowing all they needed to wake in the light was there in them

There were so many of these gray ones and I watched many of them
I saw them touch the one with dreams and they brought away nothing
As the golden ones touched them, the glow only flickered and then died
Fogs without substance echoed with the sound of wasted wishes, intent
False excuses given so reality was never faced thus required no courage

"If I can love someone enough they will love me back or change"
"He/she said they loved me" "He/she can't be married and lead me on"
"Giving my kids everything they want won't hurt them at all"
"If I get hit just one more time, then I'll leave"
"The kids don't really see what is happening with us"
And on, and on, and on, the illusions build, and fog deepens even more

I turned ever slowly to look in the mirror, to see what veil surrounded me
Almost afraid to see there was a gray fog there, an illusion built to hide in
But I knew my soul had found peace at last and I openly shared my love
So I smiled and opened my eyes to find shining a great golden glow
And there behind me, I could have sworn, I saw an angel wink at me
As time returned, I wondered, if others could see their veils, would they

◆

The question was asked in conversation, "I was told life began at 40, they lied! And now they tell me it begins at 50, just when does life begin?" I am sure many ask that very question...so I thought...and these were my thoughts...

When Does Life Begin?

Age comes drifting in silently and all too swiftly to all of us
The clock no longer ticks and tocks but now seems to spin
Days fly by all too quickly, and merge into months vanished
And as the seasons of spring, summer, fall and winter come
We related to each as they pass, according to where we are
Not in terms of location, but where we are in the lives we live

Exactly where does one's life begin? At 30, at 40 or even at 50?
Life begins when you finally step back, and find who you are
Each year is another season of life, and of lessons to be learned
The impetuousness of the young, of the spring, blooming wildly
While summer brings a relaxation into the things spring found
Fall is the retrospective time when what we have done sinks in
Winter is the soft covering of knowledge of time savored or wasted

Life begins when we decide to live it, and age only helps us see
The seasons within ourselves determine how we bloom, not the years
Is there less appreciation of the sunrises because we age, or more
The real wonder of a child is not always seen by young, new parents
As we age, we find that in the eyes of babies is the innocence we wish for
To be able to begin again to see as we should have, and not as we have
To to be able to reach out blindly in love, and have it always returned
Perhaps the joys of life are like the colors we see throughout our life
The brilliant vibrant colors jumping out at us seen with youthful eyes
Now take on richer, deeper overtones, and meanings we begin to savor

Do not fret for you think the excitement of youth is no longer to be found
The excitement is still there, all around you, only now it has more meaning
Instead of overwhelming you and rushing past you, it can now linger on

To be tasted fully, and then, instead of being discarded, passed to another
When does life begin...it begins each day...a new chance to feel all things
To be the person you want to be...to see and feel all the good around you
To ignore the bad, for the bad always passes in time and should be forgotten
And to find, in all the world, there is only one you...and you are worth love

◆

Where Home Is

Yesterday I was out visiting some people, enjoying the friendship
As I got up to leave I said, "I guess it is time go home"
While I was driving I began to wonder, just where home really is
Pulling into my drive located in the country on a couple of acres
To a home of sorts. This was where I lived but it was not home
Not anymore than the many places and houses I had lived before

Places of only brief refuge from the worries and troubles of the world
Made personal and private by one's own tastes and hidden fantasies
For some a showplace of great perfection the blind would never see
Made for admiring, not for living lest it all be disturbed, out of place
Saying see, here, this is my perfect life, built as only I want it to be
For others it is just a place to be for awhile, valuing it only as such

But where then is home; is it where we grew up, the house we lived in
For many this brings mixed reactions, for all the happy homes existing
There were so many unhappy homes where life's beginnings were hard
Are both home. We call them both home. Where does the difference lie
In that place you hide from others where memories good and bad live
open the door of time and reach in and remember your own panorama
Was it truly your home, or was it just the place you happened to be raised

Home. Such a magical word of so many definitions, of fact and of mind
Could it be just a mythical place we carry in dreams, ever searching for
I have been home many times in my life, both in person and in memory
Yet few of these were ever in the same physical place, or even in time
But in the true sense of the word, I was home, I was where I belonged

For home is not a place, to be truly home is a sensation felt by the heart
Home can only be found where love is. Not partial love, nor controlling love
But only where true love and acceptance of one's self worth is welcomed
In those arms were I am loved then I am truly home, if only for a little while
A home more real to me than a castle, for it is here, only here I feel safe
For you see I know home, the real home we all return to is just that, love
And since that is so, how can anywhere be called home where love is not

Home is not a place of physical dimensions yet we can own it just as well
We carry the essence of home with us wherever we go deep inside a heart
Watching the joy in someone as they see us arrive are we not home again
To see the love light shine ever so deeply in another's eyes are we not home
Wrapped gently in arms of love is a home of the finest grandest palace of life
To go home is not to go to a place, it is to go to where your heart is at peace
Your are lost in the space between heartbeats, where time has no meaning
Breath is of vibrations instead of air, silence becomes as beautiful music
And ever so softly the melody plays on the soul...if only for a while

◆

Which Day Is It?

The darkness slowly and reluctantly relinquishes its hold on the night
Great warm rays of light spread out like fingers reaching over the earth
Leisurely awakening begins and awareness of the weekend celebration
Our country of freedom, justice and liberty heralds Independence Day
Yet in the midst of the observance and festivities are shadows of chains
For many the holiday observance mirrors a sinister, darker, connotation

While the eyes of the country are on the waving flag of Independence Day
Singing out songs of wars fought, precious freedoms, treasured liberties
And lamenting the glorious sacrifices made so all could be free to choose
Within the country itself, within the very families for which it was all fought
Lie the injustices, greed, control making today no different than the rest
The name of the day is the same just written differently…In Dependence Day

Yet this holiday, Independence Day should be a great shining example
Held out for all to see, the truth is there in the billowing flag in the wind
This nation would not be here, could never exist, without some sacrifice
The founders could not live with the oppression and control and spoke out
Although they were put down time and time again they needed to be free
Along with the fears they had, they also felt this all the way into their souls

They understood, captivity, control, abuse, only feeds more of the same
And the longer they waited the more ingrained the pattern on generations
Until virtual slavery was an acceptable thing, becoming a slave or a controller
They fought with everything they had just so their children could live free
Now the question is, can you do the same, or do we take down your flag
What price have you put on freedom, on self worth, on your kids, on love

Thousands gave their very lives just so you could be free to make a choice
Justification of control, abuse, hurt, broken hearts is the refuge of cowards
Those who refuse to see small eyes growing and watching your flag burn
Like our country there is a price to be paid, but what price is freedom worth
The price of self worth and being loved? Each must answer for themselves
But never, never forget, the price you pay, children continue to pay…forever

Which is it? Independence Day or In Dependence Day…it is your choice

♦

Poetry and music are the notes

of the melody of our hearts

Only Forward

Wishes, dreams and memories
Past, present and future
All indistinguishable in the moment
Stretching out into forever
Touch that part where love lives in the silence
Ever reaching out to seek just a thread
of the robe once wrapped all too completely around
Yet the light cannot shine out lest the source be from within
It is we who make the threads of the robe
And light the candle that burns with the light of the son
Consuming us in its magnificent flame
Do I dream, or am I there
One never knows for sure
But the heart can glow as the soul soars in that tiny
Yet forever moment
While uncontrolled tears of joy flow freely in release
I have touched the sky
I can never go back
Only forward

◆

Where the spirit walks there are no footprints
but the path is always shown to those who
look with their hearts and seek to see

Someone once asked, "How come the gals on the TV and movies look gorgeous together in the shower and most of us average folks just look like drowned rats? What's their secret? And can it be bought?" This was my answer...

Perception

Ah the secret is in the perceived sensualness of what is done

The gift of the mind to the heart of exactly where one really is

Where the water is from a waterfall in the middle of the forest

The light showing from a golden moon balanced in the heavens

As you stand embraced together in the tide pool covered in mist

The slickness of the flesh amplified by the flow the water over it

Feeling the bodies touch no longer in friction but now in waves

Sliding over one another slowly savoring the sensual sensations

The waters rush washing away all hidden silent inhibitions

The mind dances the image of the who you always wanted to be

For now, while the water hides and yet enhances it is who you are

As you come together you are the very essence of all perfect love

And as the time ends and you begin to towel the body of the water

If you do not look in the mirror, the memory remains, and you smile

And once more, for a just a time, you were again young and perfect

◆

In the moments of choice,

of indecision, of questions, if you listen,

you can hear whispers on the wind

softly blowing the answers into you as you breathe in

Savor them, feel them, taste them

Let them become part of you before you breathe out

...and they are lost again

A Thank You and a Wish for You

Thoughts jumbled and scattered tumble in my mind as I search for words

Words to express so much in so little time and space here at the end

Traditional endings seem meaningless and cliché even though real and true

What would I wish for all of you, for you are all different, yet all alike

What has touched one has touched another, those not yet touched, will be

For none escapes the pain of learning, of others, of life, of themselves

To experience the true meaning of love, the touch of forgiveness

The awakening of one's own heart to the purpose of their being

The overwhelming joy of walking surrounded by angels and light

Yes, I have it…my friends…with all my love

I wish you my dreams

◆

A Gift for the Reader

Wind Whisperings hopes you have enjoyed reading this book as much as we have enjoyed publishing it for you. If you have any comments or suggestions, please use the form here to let us know what you think.

Book Comments _____

_____

_____

_____

_____

☐ Please notify me of any new books by Lastmanout.
  (Those who send in this page will receive 10% off any new book.)

☐ I would like to order a copy of Soul Cries on CD, normally $12.95 but with this page only $10.95.

☐ I have been to Lastmanout's Soul Cries web site.

☐ I have been to the www.windwhispering.com web site

☐ I purchased this book at _____

Web Site Comments: _____

_____

_____

_____

Name: _____

Address: _____

City _____

State _____ Zip _____

Note: Photocopies not acceptable. This page must be returned for reader discount to be applied to CDs or any new Lastmanout book.